THINK DIFFERENTLY

NOTHING IS DIFFERENT UNTIL YOU THINK DIFFERENTLY

BIBLE STUDY

JAMES MACDONALD

LifeWay Press®
Nashville, Tennessee

CONTENTS

THE AUTHOR

JAMES MACDONALD has committed his life to the unapologetic proclamation of God's Word. He is the founder and senior pastor of Harvest Bible Chapel, one of the fastest-growing churches in the Chicago area, reaching more than 13,000 lives each weekend. Heard on the "Walk in the Word" radio and television broadcasts, his practical teaching is also accessed by thousands online. Through James's leadership and by God's grace, Harvest Bible Fellowship, the church-planting ministry he founded in 2002, has planted more than one hundred churches across North America and around the world.

Born in London, Ontario, Canada, James received his master's degree from Trinity Evangelical Divinity School in Deerfield, Illinois, and his doctorate from Phoenix Seminary. He and his wife, Kathy, have three adult children and reside in Chicago. For more information about James and these ministries, visit *www.harvestbible.org* or *www.walkintheword.org*.

Other books and Bible studies by James MacDonald:

Always True: God's Promises When Life Is Hard
Bible study (LifeWay, 2011)

Always True: God's Five Promises for When Life

Is Hard (Moody, 2011)

Authentic: Developing the Disciplines of a Sincere Faith Bible study (LifeWay, 2013)

Authentic (Moody, 2013)

Come Home (Moody, 2013)

Downpour: He Will Come to Us like the Rain Bible study (LifeWay, 2006)

Downpour: He Will Come to Us like the Rain (B&H, 2006)

God Wrote a Book (Crossway, 2002)

Gripped by the Greatness of God Bible study (LifeWay, 2005)

Gripped by the Greatness of God (Moody, 2005)

Have the Funeral small-group study (LifeWay, 2011)

Lord, Change Me (Moody, 2012)

Lord, Change My Attitude Bible study (LifeWay, 2008)

Lord, Change My Attitude ... Before It's Too Late (Moody, 2001)

Seven Words to Change Your Family (Moody, 2001)

10 Choices: A Proven Plan to Change Your Life Forever (Thomas Nelson, 2008)

When Life Is Hard Bible study (LifeWay, 2010)

When Life Is Hard (Moody, 2010)

Vertical Church Bible study (LifeWay, 2012)

Vertical Church (David C Cook, 2012)

Act Life a Man (Moody, 2014)

Visit *www.lifeway.com/jamesmacdonald* for information about James MacDonald resources published by LifeWay.

THINK
DIFFERENTLY

INTRODUCTION

A long time ago I memorized Proverbs 23:7, "As [a man] thinks in his heart, so is he" (NKJV). When you think about it, that statement is the ultimate no-brainer. Thinking determines outcome more than anything else. Our actions, attitudes, and self-awareness all flow from the way we think.

This is a study about the way our thinking influences everything we do. This is true even when we are dealing with God and what God asks us to do. We need to ask ourselves what happens when we make decisions or promises but haven't changed our underlying thinking.

We have a long way to go in these sessions and we're only beginning to grapple with the truth that nothing is really different until we think differently. At this point, are you content with your old arguments, old opinions, old mindsets, and old patterns? Or, do you find yourself leaning into the possibility of a different, God-centered way of thinking?

I would just like to say prophetically and prayerfully that this series is going to change us. May these weeks be a time when God shows us from His Word that real change ultimately means thinking differently. According to Proverbs 23:7, the way we think in our hearts is the way we are.

HOW TO GET THE MOST FROM THIS STUDY

1. Attend each group experience.
   - → Watch the DVD teaching.
   - → Participate in the group discussions.

2. Complete the content in this workbook.
   - → Read the daily lessons.
   - → Complete the learning activities.
   - → Memorize each week's suggested memory verse.
   - → Watch for window-rattling, earth-shattering, life-altering encounters with God's revealed glory and manifest presence.

WEEK 1

WHY IT IS SO HARD TO THINK DIFFERENTLY?

Welcome to this group discussion of Think Differently.

Make introductions within in the group. Take a few minutes to approach the theme of *Think Differently*. Talk together about what it means to change your mind. One of the phrases you will hear repeated frequently in this series is, "Nothing is different until you think differently." Use the following questions to expand the discussion. Encourage everyone to participate.

Describe a life experience that involved changing your mind.

What were the benefits you experienced as a result of changing your mind?

What were some negatives that could have happened if you had not changed your mind?

This is a study about the way our thinking influences everything we do. This is true even when we are dealing with God and what God asks us to do. We need to ask ourselves what happens when we make decisions or promises but haven't changed our underlying thinking.

To prepare for the first teaching video in this series, read the following verses aloud in unison:

> *For though we walk in the flesh, we are not waging war according to the flesh. For the weapons of our warfare are not of the flesh but have divine power to destroy strongholds. We destroy arguments and every lofty opinion raised against the knowledge of God, and take every thought captive to obey Christ, being ready to punish every disobedience, when your obedience is complete.*
> **2 CORINTHIANS 10:3-6**

WATCH

COMPLETE THE VIEWER GUIDE BELOW AS YOU WATCH DVD SESSION 1.

Why is it so hard to change my thinking?

Because my battles are not primarily _____ (v. 3).

There are at least five major mental battles:

1. _____
2. _____
3. _____
4. _____
5. _____

Because my weapons are not readily _____ (v. 4).

Our immediate tendency is to rely on _____ weapons. .

The weapons God provides for us have the following qualities:

They are _____.

They are _____.

They _____ strongholds.

Because my _____ are not easily _____ (v. 5).

My old _____ made sense.

My old _____ felt good.

My old _____ is opposed to _____.

My old _____ comes naturally.

Because my engagement must be _____ (v. 6).

DISCUSS THE VIDEO SEGMENT WITH YOUR GROUP.

Of the four reasons James gave for the difficulty of being able to think differently, which made the most sense to you? Why?

When James talked about "flesh-weapons," what weapons in your arsenal stood out to you? When do you find yourself using those weapons?

When he introduced the idea of mental wars and spiritual warfare, James described five areas where we battle: behaviors, relationships, finances, ideology, and morality. Which of these areas seems most like a constant battleground for you?

Based on this session's teaching, how would you say your thinking affects your victory or defeat in your life? How does this evaluation fit with the challenge James gave: "This is where your best thinking has gotten you"?

In what ways would you say the teaching for this session has given you hope?

Application: We have a long way to go in these sessions, and we're only beginning to grapple with the truth that nothing is really different until we think differently. At this point, are you content with your old arguments, old opinions, old mindsets, and old patterns? Or, do you find yourself leaning into the possibility of a different, God-centered way of thinking? Take a few minutes with the group and pray with each other asking for God's help in learning to think differently during these weeks.

This week's Scripture memory:

As [a man] thinks in his heart, so is he. **PROVERBS 23:7, NKJV**

Assignment: Complete the daily lessons for next week in preparation for the next group experience. Make a note of further questions or thoughts related to this week's teaching that you can share with other group members. Pray for each member of your group by name. Ask God to help them think differently this week.

WHY IS IT SO HARD TO THINK DIFFERENTLY?

A long time ago I memorized Proverbs 23:7, "As [a man] thinks in his heart, so is he" (NKJV). When you think about it, that statement is the ultimate no-brainer. Thinking determines outcome more than anything else. Our actions, attitudes, and self-awareness all flow from the way we think.

For almost thirty years now I've been drilling on this matter of behavior. I've been praying, preaching, watching, and waiting for people to change. In the late 1990's, I first taught a series eventually called *Lord, Change Me*. The messages focused on lessons from Romans 6 and 7. We were asking: *When I get to a fork in the road, why do I always say yes to temptation? Why can't I say yes to God? How do I say no to temptation and yes to God*? And, we learned that change never happens without God's help. As the apostle Paul, the writer of Romans, summarized it, "Wretched man that I am! Who will deliver me from this body of death? Thanks be to God through Jesus Christ our Lord!" (Rom. 7:24-25a).

But as I kept thinking and praying about change, asking the Lord to change me as well as our church, I realized I had to get to a deeper level on the subject. Right around 2002, I preached a series titled, *Lord, Change My Attitude, Before It's Too Late*. It was a study of five terminally self-destructive attitudes displayed by the people of Israel in the Book of Numbers: complaining, coveting, criticizing, doubting, and rebelling, alongside five God-honoring attitudes that can replace each of the negative ones: thanksgiving, being content, loving, exercising faith, and submitting. The core truth we were confronting is that attitudes are patterns of thinking formed over a long period of time that must be replaced. With God's help, we put off the old and put on the new.

Still, challenging and changing an attitude doesn't necessarily address where attitudes come from. So, I've been wrestling with what really has to change if behavior is going to change, which brings us to this study, *Think Differently*. We're about to face the reality that nothing is going to change until we think differently. This first week, we are simply confronting the truth that changing the way we think is one of the hardest tasks any of us can take on. We definitely need God's help.

I would just like to say prophetically and prayerfully that this series is going to change us. May these weeks be a time when God shows us from His Word that real change ultimately means thinking differently. According to Proverbs 23:7, the way we think in our hearts is the way we are.

DAY 1
WINNING AND LOSING IN THE MIND

If you're like most of us, you have probably been baffled by someone's words or actions. Why does Bill lose his temper and yell at his wife? Why does she respond by having a third glass of wine every evening to dull her pain? Why is their daughter deeply involved in risky behavior that never delivers what she is looking for? Why do your own words and actions leave you wondering why certain situations trigger humiliating or hurtful responses from you?

The reason is the way they—and you—think. God's Word states the problem in Proverbs 27:3, but Scripture also gives us direction and powerful hope in these verses:

> *For though we walk in the flesh, we are not waging war according to the flesh. For the weapons of our warfare are not of the flesh but have divine power to destroy strongholds. We destroy arguments and every lofty opinion raised against the knowledge of God, and take every thought captive to obey Christ, being ready to punish every disobedience, when your obedience is complete.*
>
> **2 CORINTHIANS 10:3-6**

Underline or circle every word in these verses that you want to understand better. Summarize your initial response to this passage by writing at least one question you want answered during this study.

OUR SITUATION

If just changing the way we think causes real change, the lasting change, and the big change—why aren't more people changing? Here's why: Because it is terrifically difficult to change the way you or I, or anyone, thinks. Second Corinthians 10:3-6 helps us not only see why changing our minds is difficult it also shows us how God wants to help us in the process.

Take a moment to pray about your participation in this study. Ask God for an open heart and mind—a willingness to change as He works in you. Then ask God to show you one or more areas where you may need to start thinking differently. Sit quietly and write down below any areas that come to mind.

This week we're going to review four reasons that explain why it's hard to change our thinking. Let's start by looking closely at the current state of our thinking. In order to do that, let's revisit several other examples mentioned in the video lesson.

Why does Kevin blow up every relationship that gets too close to him? Because he believes proximity equals pain. That's what he thinks. So as he moves close to a person, eventually he'll find a way to wreck the relationship because he doesn't want someone to get close enough to hurt him.

Is he right about that? No, he's wrong. It is the way he thinks. Part of him longs for intimacy with others, yet the fear of pain part of him always interrupts and destroys his relationships. And nothing will be different until he thinks differently. You may see a lot of yourself in Kevin. Or, maybe you struggle in other areas.

Why is Kim so secretive and so private? Why is she so afraid to make herself known? Because she has been rejected in the past and she doesn't want to experience it again. She thinks keeping all her superficial relationships will protect her. Is she right? No, but her actions are flowing from her thinking. Nothing will be different until she thinks differently. Until then, to paraphrase Proverbs 27:3, as Kim thinks in her heart, so is she.

It's hard to question our own thoughts. They must be right, right? But maybe not. The fact is, we think wrong thoughts all the time. And often, having them challenged and corrected is a gift that rescues us from ourselves.

Complete the following statements:

I once thought lying was a useful way to get out of trouble. Then ...

I once thought being an adult would be easy. Then ...

I once thought I was good enough to deserve entry into heaven. Then ...

Maybe there is dysfunction is in your family and the way they think distorts or blocks efforts to be loving toward each other. You might be asking, "When is my dad going to stop with all of the stoic stupidity and start telling me he loves me? I think he feels it, but why can't he say it?"

Well, there are some things going on in the way your father thinks about being that open. People say, "I love you," all the time, but he thinks that saying "I love you" is an awkward vulnerability he can't handle. You may be able to press him on Christmas Eve and get the words out, but they're not going to flow freely the way you want them to until he actually starts to think differently about expressing what he feels.

After reading the following examples, consider how each of them is going to have to change their thinking. How are they a product of what they are thinking in their heart?

Linda is hypercritical.

Lance is lazy. He changes jobs like most people change their socks.

Lisa is an overeater.

Lyle is an overachiever.

Larry is complaining every minute of the day.

Lou is losing to sexual temptation.

Lauren is once more leaving her loved ones in the lurch.

Why? Are those things right? No, but simply telling them "this is wrong; this is what's right" isn't going to fix it. Take it from someone who spends his entire life saying to people, "Not this. This," but unless the change happens at the thinking level, external conformity will only be short-lived.

DAY 2
BATTLES BEYOND THE PHYSICAL

As we explore 2 Corinthians 10:3-6, which is what I consider to be the most concentrated passage in the New Testament about our ways of thinking, let's keep an important question in mind: If a change in thinking is the way to make lasting change, why aren't more people changing?

It can be hard to change the way people think. Don't you agree? In the Day 1 assignment you had a chance to begin seeing that your mind, like mine, has some deep thinking ruts that are hard to get out of. And, if your response to me saying that it's hard to change your thinking is, "James, I change my mind all the time. In fact, I change my mind multiple times every day," let me point out that you are describing a troublesome way of thinking, not a change of thinking. Continually changing your mind is a pattern the Bible calls "double-mindedness" (see Jas. 1:7-8). That's a pattern of thinking that stubbornly resists change. This study can help you confront this pattern of thinking. Let's think about the particular difficulty Paul laid out in 2 Corinthians 10:3:

> *For though we walk in the flesh, we are not waging war according to the flesh.*

What are some of the obvious differences to you between the pictures of "walking" and of "waging war"?

The Corinthian Christians seem to be especially challenged by walking in their faith. As a congregation, they could be a sexually-indulgent church, overlooking or excusing sin as well as behaving sinfully in other ways. Conflicts and false teachings caused more problems in their church. In his letter, Paul reminded the Corinthians that the Christian life is about battles that are not primarily physical.

The word *walk* was used more than thirty times by Paul as a way of referring to living or moving through life. This means we can usually substitute the word *live* where we read the word *walk* in verses like Galatians 5:16, "But I say, walk by the Spirit [live by the Spirit], and you will not gratify the desires of the flesh," and Ephesians 4:1, "I therefore, a prisoner for the Lord, urge you to walk [live] in a manner worthy of the calling to which you have been called."

Why is walking a good way to describe moving through life?

In 2 Corinthians 10:3, Paul also used the word *flesh* twice. It's the Greek word *sarx* that the Bible sometimes uses to refer to your old, sinful nature. But here it simply means your body, your physical reality, your way of dealing with things.

Do you understand that you are not just a physical being? There is a part of you that will live forever—with God or separated from Him, based on what you do about the offer of salvation to you from His Son, Jesus Christ. The most important part of you is not the physical part. The most important part of you is made up of your mind, emotions, and will, all of which compose your soul. If you're saved, that part of you, your soul, is the part of you that will live forever with God.

What are some examples in your own experience that convince you that you are not just a physical being? How do you know you have a soul?

When Paul said, "For though we walk in the flesh," he meant that even though we live our lives in this physical reality, we are not primarily fighting a physical battle. The reason why *primarily* is there is because we need to acknowledge the real physical problems that affect our lives. For example, one of the mistakes that Christians make when they start talking about thinking is that Christians are famous for not acknowledging the reality of mental illness. Mental illness is real. If you have a mental illness, just as when you have a physical illness, it's time to see a physician. Once you take away any problems around you that are physical (flesh problems), many of the rest will have to do with the way you think. Those thinking battles can create your mental wars. Here are some of the battlefronts:

BEHAVIORAL

Your and my behavior can feel and look physical, but our behaviors may be coming from the way we think. You may be battling various behaviors in yourself and in others, but nothing will change much until your thinking changes—not for you or those you love.

What is one behavior battle you know you've been losing?

RELATIONAL

You may think that you should never admit when you're wrong or that you have to be perfect. Maybe you can't see that your behavior is hurting others. Maybe the way that you relate to others is working against what you long to experience in relationships.

How are your current relationships affected by the way you think?

FINANCIAL

Do you think that money and things will increase your happiness? Check out Philippians 4:12-13.

I know how to be brought low, and I know how to abound. In any and every circumstance, I have learned the secret of facing plenty and hunger, abundance and need. I can do all things through him who strengthens me.

Happiness is in no way tethered to what you have or don't have. Describe one financial issue that feels like a battle to you right now.

IDEOLOGICAL

Ideology is your filter through which you interpret reality. Every person has an ideology, a mix of many different aspects of thinking. Another term for this is worldview.

When you describe your basic outlook on life, what three or four terms do you use?

MORAL

Moral thinking involves questions. Is there a right and wrong? Can sin be resisted or is it inevitable? Can sin be defeated, atoned for, and forgiven? Our thoughts about meaning and purpose in life fall into this area.

What has shaped your thinking about the central themes of life?

I'm asking you to embrace a certain truth. It is that the battle for your priorities— for your prodigal child, for better prospects in your marriage, for better prospects in your life, all of those battles—are shaped, won, or lost by the way you we think.

Take a moment to thank God today for opening your eyes to the truth that your thinking affects everything else. Continue to ask Him to help you think differently.

DAY 3

WEAPONS OUT OF REACH

As soon as Paul said that our warfare is not primarily physical, he went on to warn us in the next verse that our weapons are not readily accessible.

> *For the weapons of our warfare are not of the flesh but have divine power to destroy strongholds.*
> **2 CORINTHIANS 10:4**

This verse tells us there are weapons to help you change your thinking. The term *warfare* here literally means our strategy for the campaign. But there's a problem: The real weapons are not readily accessible weapons. The arsenal on hand, the one that we tend to depend on, is actually the most ineffective. It is our set of flesh weapons.

Don't forget this: When our first thought in a spiritual battle is to reach for our flesh weapons, the war is already lost.

What might be the problem with using flesh weapons in nonflesh warfare?

Do you want to know what qualifies as flesh weapons? They are the desires of the flesh. Galatians 5:16-17 tells us this:

> *But I say, walk by the Spirit, and you will not gratify the desires of the flesh. For the desires of the flesh are against the Spirit, and the desires of the Spirit are against the flesh, for these are opposed to each other, to keep you from doing the things you want to do.*

Make no mistake, there is a war going on between the physical and the non-physical. It's a battle. What does Galatians 5 tell us about the nature of flesh weapons?

Remember what Jesus said to the disciples:

The spirit indeed is willing, but the flesh is weak.
MATTHEW 26:41

The flesh is weak in terms of resisting sin but strong in terms of demanding its own way. There isn't a person whose heart is sincere who wouldn't say that his or her behavior doesn't always match what he or she believes to be true. That person is NOT fully living what he or she believes to be true.

So, here a list if some of the flesh weapons:

Now the works of the flesh are evident: sexual immorality, impurity, sensuality, idolatry, sorcery, enmity, strife, jealousy, fits of anger, rivalries, dissensions, divisions, envy, drunkenness, orgies, and things like these. I warn you, as I warned you before, that those who do such things will not inherit the kingdom of God.
GALATIANS 5:19-21

How many weapons did Paul mention specifically in this passage?

How could a couple of these be used as weapons against others?

We use flesh weapons to react to offenses or to act in offensive ways. They are readily available to us and we think of them as effective ways to defend ourselves. They are not. And if those patterns go on in your life uninterrupted, you're sinning. You're not serving God. The proof of salvation is the progress in our sanctification, becoming more like Christ.

When we are describing God's work in sanctifying and changing us, we often say, "Not perfectly, but increasingly this is the Lord's work in changing me. It starts with changing my mind."

You just read the statement, "The proof of the salvation is the progress in our sanctification." How does your life currently demonstrate how God is doing the work He started in you with your salvation?

Now that we've looked at the flesh weapons that are at hand but useless, let's think a little about the effective weapons God offers to us. Second Corinthians 10:4 is a little frustrating here.

For the weapons of our warfare are not of the flesh but have divine power to destroy strongholds.

I thought that Paul would tell us what the weapons are, but he doesn't list our weapons because he wanted his readers to stay focused on how effective these weapons are. Our awareness of weaponry comes from elsewhere in Scripture. In Ephesians 6:10-17 we find all this defensive armor, but the only weapon to win the battle in your mind is what verse 17 calls "the sword of the Spirit, which is the word of God."

The first way I change my thinking is the renewing of my mind (see Rom. 12:2). The Bible calls it in Ephesians 5:26 "the washing...with the word." The Word of God cleanses our thinking. You have to have the sword of the Spirit.

In 2 Corinthians 6:7, Paul talked about the "weapons of righteousness" we have. We have the righteousness of Jesus: "Not having a righteousness of my own that comes from the law, but that which comes through faith in Christ," (Phil. 3:9). It's the fact that no matter where you've been—or no matter what you've done, or no matter what you regret—if you have turned from your sin and embraced Jesus Christ by faith, your Creator God, through your faith in His Son Jesus, declares you to be righteous. He sees you as righteous. The righteousness of Jesus becomes our "weapons of righteousness."

We take up the weapons of Christ's righteousness by faith in Him. As John declared, "And this is the victory that has overcome the world—our faith" (1 John 5:4). Nothing will get your thinking to a better place than rejecting what seems to you to be true and embracing what God declares to be true. Turn away from your righteousness as a useless flesh weapon and take up the righteousness of Christ, a weapon which cannot be overcome.

What does it mean to, by faith, take up the righteousness of Christ rather than relying on your own? In what situations are you doing that right now?

The weapons, from 2 Corinthians 10:4, that God has given us are:

- **"DIVINE":** The word *divine* with the word *power* literally means the weapons that God has given us to change our thinking are from God. God is the source of the weapons.

- **"POWERFUL":** These weapons are powerful. The word translated *power* is the word from which we get our word *dynamite*. These are powerful weapons. The problem is that we may not believe that the weapons God has given us are actually powerful, and we think that we need flesh weapons to solve our problems. We must change our thinking.

- **"ABLE TO DESTROY STRONGHOLDS":** The word *strongholds* is sometimes translated *fortresses*. This is how Paul described the ways of thinking that keep you from the life that God wants you. Strongholds are fortified mental positions, which we will storm in the sessions to come.

When you think about God offering weapons to defeat internal and external attacks, how hard is it for you to believe and act on that offer?

God doesn't want to trim your strongholds or to limit the effects of your strongholds. The picture here is of a wrecking ball swinging into a tower. Some translations even say demolish. The ways of thinking that are keep us in our strongholds, isolated from what God has for us, must be destroyed.

DAY 4

DAUNTING STRONGHOLDS

If destroying strongholds were easy, everyone would do it. Most people have their thinking so deeply entrenched by the time they're into their second decade of adulthood that they don't change after that. They might change jobs. They might change churches. They might change marriages. But they don't change their thinking. Yet, they're shocked to find the exact same stuff tends to keep happening to them. Why? Because a lot more of our own thinking guides our lives than we are ever really willing to acknowledge.

> **Briefly review the last several years of your life. What negative patterns can you see? In what areas have you been trying to make changes, only to keep getting the same bad results? These are clues to strongholds.**

MY OLD ARGUMENTS MADE SENSE TO ME.

In 2 Corinthians 10:5, Paul described the effect of the weapons God provides. They destroy arguments. *Arguments* mean reasonings—our reasons for our actions. However, deeply entrenched patterns of thinking also often become reasons why we do what we do.

- The man who robs the bank.

- The spouse who chooses to cheat.

- The kid who lies.

- The business owner who embezzles.

- The church member who spreads strife.

- The Christian who lives in stubborn independence from the Savior he says he trusts.

We all have our reasons or arguments, but strongholds don't get destroyed until those arguments are refuted and torn down.

When in your life has a longstanding bad habit or pattern been broken? In what ways can you now see that your freedom came because you started thinking differently?

MY OLD OPINIONS FELT GOOD.

God wants to destroy the wrong thinking in you and me. Second Corinthians 10:5 says, "We destroy arguments and every lofty opinion..."

Do you have some lofty opinions of yourself? What positions have you taken that you're convinced you could never step away from.

Proverbs 3:7 says, "Be not wise in your own eyes." It is very human to be overly confident in our own thinking. And, honestly, Christians can be the most strident, the most difficult, the most inflexible, and the most insistent that they are right about things. Our lives aren't sideways because we're arguing with someone about who Jesus Christ is or if the Bible is God's Word. The problem is that we've taken that doctrinal certainty and applied it to so many issues about which we could be deferential, reasonable, and measured. But somehow we're not. Lofty opinions feel good. They are the false comforts of flesh weapons.

When have you recently been willing to set aside a long-held opinion because you realized it wasn't the only way to look at reality?

BECAUSE MY OLD MIND IS OPPOSED TO GOD.

Paul tells us that our arguments and lofty opinions are actually aimed "against the knowledge of God" (2 Cor. 10:5). At the end of the day, these bad reasons, these old arguments, and these lofty opinions oppose God. That will not change until we see it like it is. When we oppose God's work, we are opposing God Himself. Jesus suffered our pain to free us from sin. Sin only causes pain in the end. Sin doesn't help. It isn't good. It may bring pleasure for a moment, but in the end it destroys. If we think differently, our behavior will change. That's what the gospel is all about.

BECAUSE MY OLD PATTERN COMES NATURALLY.

Second Corinthians 10:5 continues, "...and take every thought captive to obey Christ." Every thought that doesn't go with the knowledge of God will be taken prisoner. They will be taken off the field of battle of our minds. Those thoughts will submit to the Lordship of Christ.

> **How many thoughts do you think in a day that you didn't consciously decide to think? What happens when you show your thoughts who is really in charge?**

Until noncaptive thinking changes, nothing else is going to change. Noncaptive thoughts are actually lofty opinions, an old way of thinking that feels good to us but opposes God. We have to take that thought captive. We have to decide: No more unfiltered thoughts. No more unapproved, unchallenged, where-did-that-come-from thoughts. Every thought is going to get reviewed.

I found myself driving with my wife this morning thinking about something. Kathy asked, "What are you thinking about?" I didn't want to tell her because she has already said, "You have to let that go!" So I just said, "I'm not thinking about it anymore." I took that thought captive to the obedience of Christ.

The thought was not defensible, biblical, or helpful. It had to go. It had to be taken prisoner. It can't get into my head unfiltered and unchosen. It must be rejected. It must be if I'm going to get to a better place—but my old pattern comes so naturally and so easily.

DAY 5
PERSONAL ENGAGEMENT

I remember about five or six years ago, I was going through a really tough few months. I was struggling even to preach. I was really wrestling with some things, so I called up a guy, a Christian man, who counsels people. He had been a friend to me in various ways, so we arranged a time to talk. What he said changed my life.

I told him the story, saying something like, "Well, I did this and then this happened. So I did this, and then THIS happened. NOW look where I am. What is going to change this? How can this be different? I never intended for this mess to happen." And he said, "Well, James, this is where your best thinking has gotten you." BAM! That is an awesome insight.

> **Before going on, meditate on that statement for a few minutes. Based on what you've learned so far in this week, how is the statement, "This is where your best thinking has gotten you," helpful to you?**

We are not actively and intentionally trying to hurt ourselves. We're not trying to make our lives miserable. I'm sure you would never say, "My main goal this month is to get as unhappy as possible!" Most people aren't working on that; most people are working on the opposite. If it's not happening like you know it could be happening, embrace this reality: You are where your best thinking has gotten you.

Maybe you're in a place where it's going to take you some time. I'm just trying to show you the road map here. If you're where your best thinking as gotten you, then you're going to need some better thinking.

You may be feeling a little overwhelmed right now, having second thoughts about thinking differently. Strongholds resist being questioned or called into doubt. If there are situations in your life that just flared under the weight of ,"You are where your best thinking has gotten you," it is a good time to lean into God's love for you. Being confronted or corrected can include a lot of grace even in the discomfort.

In Psalm 139:23-24 David concluded an amazing prayer with a specific request: "Search me, O God, and know my heart! Try me and know my thoughts! And see if there be any grievous way in me, and lead me in the way everlasting!" As you pray through these verses, put them into your own language and express your heart.

No one can think different thoughts for you. I'm encouraging you to pour yourself into this series, to do the same and to take part in every session during of this study. Then you'll look back at how God changed your life as He helped you to think differently.

That's why Paul ends our passage on thinking with these sobering words:

> *We destroy arguments ... Being ready to punish every disobedience, when your obedience is complete.*
> **2 CORINTHIANS 10:5-6**

Paul said to the Corinthians, "I'm coming. I'm going to take care of some things. We're going to correct some thinking and destroy some strongholds. But I can't do it until 'when your obedience is complete.'"

You have to do your part before anyone else can do their part. I can't change your thinking for you. You have to make it personal. You have to choose to do this your-self. No one can do this work for you.

Like me, you may have the hiccups a lot. I've heard about many different remedies through the years: Get someone to scare you (but that didn't work very well), hold your breath, drink something upside down. I've tried them all—unsuccessfully, I may add.

This week I had the hiccups so bad that the chair was rocking, and it wasn't a rocking chair. Kathy, whom I love so dearly, and in a way that only she could (because she had heard this from someone), came to me while I was hiccuping, just waiting for the next one. She said quietly, "You're calm. Let it go. You don't have the hiccups anymore." And I didn't.

Those who study the mind would tell you that the reason why there are things like this—so many different remedies around something like that—is because they work. If your mind believes that it works on something like hiccups it will work for you. And everybody swears by a different thing.

Why?

Because they believe that, and it works for them.

Obviously we have truth that is far more than subjective. I'm only just saying that there is so much power in what we think. It directs so many things that we can't even understand. We're going to have a great time studying this together and changing for God's glory as we learn to think differently.

> **Take a few minutes to pray for the people in your group as you study _Think Differently._ The strongholds each of you will be facing in the weeks to come will be daunting—that's why they are called strongholds.**

> **Ask God to show each participant that the weapons He has provided really are powerful to absolutely destroy the strongholds in order that He can direct new thinking in each of them.**

Put the initials of four people you'll be praying for specifically during this study.

1.

2.

3.

4.

WEEK 2
DESTROYING THE STRONGHOLDS IN MY DISPOSITION

Welcome back to this second session of our group discussion of Think Differently.

In our first lesson we confronted two huge aspects of our reality. First, the way we think affects the way we choose, act, and live in more ways than we realize. Second, it is very difficult to change the way we think. Take a few minutes to let people share what they have been discovering in the past week about their own thought processes and the daunting challenge of thinking differently. Use the following questions to expand the discussion while encouraging everyone to participate.

What did you find most challenging and/or helpful about the first lesson?

How have you begun to think differently about thinking?

Of the four reasons why it's hard to think differently (battles not primarily physical, weapons not readily accessible, strongholds not easily destroyable, personal engagement required), discuss the one that has affected you the most this week.

We must recognize that each us is uniquely, and in some ways unchangeably, made by our Creator.

What is one obvious and unchangeable thing about you that you can share with the group?

To prepare for this session's teaching, read the following key verses:

> *For though we walk in the flesh, we are not waging war according to the flesh. For the weapons of our warfare are not of the flesh but have divine power to destroy strongholds. We destroy arguments and every lofty opinion raised against the knowledge of God, and take every thought captive to obey Christ, being ready to punish every disobedience, when your obedience is complete.*
> **2 CORINTHIANS 10:3-6**

WATCH

COMPLETE THE VIEWER GUIDE BELOW AS YOU WATCH DVD SESSION 2.

_____ is different until we think _____.

Strongholds are _____ patterns of thinking that are stubbornly resistant to God's _____ and God's _____ for us.

The three main sources of our strongholds are:

our _____ ,

our _____ __ _____ ,

and our _____ and _____.

Everyone is born with a _____ given to you by _____.

_____ is the natural mental outlook, your predominant tendency or leaning, your prevailing point of view.

Disposition dictates my _____ pattern.

Disposition affects:

my _____-thinking,

my _____ -thinking,

my _____ -thinking,

_____ of my thinking

4 DISPOSITIONS

DISPOSITION	MAIN FOCUS	NEEDS	DOWNSIDE
Choleric			
Sanguine			
Phlegmatic			
Melancholy			

4 DISPOSITIONS

DISPOSITION	TIME	AUTHORITY	PEOPLE PROBLEM
Choleric			
Sanguine			
Phlegmatic			
Melancholy			

DISCUSS THE DVD SEGMENT WITH YOUR GROUP, USING THE QUESTIONS BELOW.

Which of the dispositions seems most like you? Since it's likely that you are primarily a combination of two of the classic dispositions, what's your runner-up disposition?

It's often easier to see the dispositions of others than to recognize our own. Discuss as a group who among you might fit each of the four categories: Choleric, Sanguine, Phlegmatic, and Melancholic.

How would you explain the difference between a personality strength and a stronghold?

In what ways do you think your disposition has shaped your faith and how you participate in your relationship with God?

Application: Seek to recognize at least one disposition stronghold you've developed. Take a few minutes with the group to pray with each other asking for God's help in learning to think differently during these weeks.

This week's Scripture memory.

We destroy arguments and every lofty opinion raised against the knowledge of God, and take every thought captive to obey Christ. **2 CORINTHIANS 10:5**

Assignment: Complete the daily lessons for this week in preparation for the next group experience. Make a note of additional questions or thoughts related to this week's teaching that you can share with other group members. Pray for each member of your group by name, asking God to help them think differently.

DESTROYING THE STRONGHOLDS IN MY DISPOSITION

Why do we want to think differently? Because nothing is different until we think differently. Once we accept this fact, we're confronted with another one: It isn't easy to think differently. All last week we examined the reasons and obstacles that keep us from changing our minds. We discovered in 2 Corinthians 10 a biblical description of our desperate situation and the battle plan God has set before us:

> *For though we walk in the flesh, we are not waging war according to the flesh. For the weapons of our warfare are not of the flesh but have divine power to destroy strongholds. We destroy arguments and every lofty opinion raised against the knowledge of God, and take every thought captive to obey Christ, being ready to punish every disobedience, when your obedience is complete.*
> **2 CORINTHIANS 10:3-6**

We concluded last week's study with the reality that we all have strongholds in our thinking. Again, we defined strongholds as fortified patterns of thinking that are stubbornly resistant to God's Word and God's will for us. They are like a walled city at the top of a mountain, able to repel any ground attack. But just as ancient walled cities cannot withstand modern warfare and air assaults, so the strongholds in our lives cannot prevail against the powerful weapons God has provided for us in this spiritual warfare.

Confronted with the fact of strongholds, it's natural to ask, "Where did strongholds come from?"

This week we're considering strongholds found in our disposition. Although we were designed by God to worship and serve Him, strongholds control God's good gifts and make them instruments for evil. So we want to destroy strongholds. We don't want to trim them. We don't want to weaken them a bit. We want to tear them down. We want to demolish the strongholds in our thinking that keep us from what God has for us. We are going to war, intent on destroying the strongholds found in our dispositions.

DAY 1

BIRTHDAY DISPOSITIONS

This entire week we are learning about the dispositions we are born with and destroying the strongholds in them. Here's the definition of dispositions that we are using: Disposition is the natural mental outlook, your predominant tendency or leaning, your prevailing point of view. For the next three weeks we're going to find all our insights by looking at the life of Jacob found in Genesis 25–50.

With your Bible sitting open at Genesis 25, let's review the setting of Jacob's birth.

> *These are the generations of Isaac, Abraham's son: Abraham fathered Isaac, and Isaac was forty years old when he took Rebekah, the daughter of Bethuel the Aramean of Paddan-aram, the sister of Laban the Aramean, to be his wife. And Isaac prayed to the LORD for his wife, because she was barren. And the LORD granted his prayer, and Rebekah his wife conceived. The children struggled together within her*
> **GENESIS 25:19-22**

After twenty years of infertility, Rebekah was going to have children. Plural. The Bible doesn't say here how many but she would have twins, at least.

Notice in verse 22 the word *struggled*. The children inside Rebekah struggled before they were born. The Hebrew here is *ratsats.* Normally the word is used to refer to crushing or oppressing. This was not that typical pregnancy experience of a child moving in the womb. Sibling rivalry was going full bore inside mom. They were at war inside her.

EVERYONE IS BORN WITH A DISPOSITION

What stories or events from your childhood give you clues about your disposition?

We all have a disposition, an outlook, a viewpoint that we are born with. Your disposition is given to you by God, who intends it for good. However, because of your sinfulness, your disposition gets bent.

Of course, some in the world believe the lie that unborn babies are just so much fetal matter. But God's Word portrays over and over that life begins at conception. So, because life begins at conception, babies in their mothers' wombs already have their dispositions, already have a plan marked out for each of them by Almighty God, and already have God's favor and purpose upon their lives.

With these two wrestling inside her, Rebekah "went to inquire of the Lord" (Gen. 25:22). What a great play, right? Anytime you're perplexed or uncertain, or anytime you don't know what to do, go to the Lord.

Stop for a moment and consider how often you respond to confusion or uncertainty by asking God for help. Would you say your default setting is more to immediately seek God's help or to try figuring things out on your own first? Why? What does that say about your disposition?

Because it was still to be written, Rebekah did not have a Bible to open. But God graciously responded in a manner that reminds us of Hebrews 11:6, "And without faith it is impossible to please him, for whoever would draw near to God must believe that he exists and that he rewards those who seek him." God rewarded Rebekah with an answer: "And the Lord said to her, 'Two nations are in your womb, and two peoples from within you shall be divided; the one shall be stronger than the other, the older shall serve the younger'" (Gen. 25:23).

These two boys about to be born were Jacob and Esau, the patriarchs of the Jews and Arabs, respectively. By the way, God's words proved true not only of the brothers but also of their offspring throughout history.

It was like that before they were born. Again, we've defined disposition as the natural mental outlook, your predominant tendency or leaning, your prevailing point of view. Disposition affects every relationship. It affects every decision. It's the filter installed on your thinking through which you process reality.

Just as four people on a street corner can watch the same accident and have different descriptions of it so you have a filter on your thinking that makes you look at all of life a certain way. It's called your temperament or personality. It's your way of thinking. It is so natural to you that you often don't even realize you're doing it.

Here's the major concern we have this week: Your strongholds are shaped by your disposition and eventually become deeply entrenched in your disposition. If you want to think differently, you have to understand not only how your disposition affects your thinking but also how the distortions and strongholds in your disposition have a vice-like grip on the way you think.

Consider how committed you are to the changes that will be required in order to think differently. What are you asking God to change about you?

Just like Jacob and Esau inside their mother, our dispositions and strongholds wrestle inside of us for control. Remember what Paul said in 2 Corinthians 10:4 about destroying strongholds and arguments. Your arguments are the reasons why you think you're right; your lofty opinions are the way you view reality and think that the way you review reality is the best way, even the right way of looking at things. What you call best and right is actually your filter, and it can become your stronghold—those reasons, those arguments, those lofty opinions. As we see them, we're asking God to demolish them in us.

Prayer this prayer:
Lord, thank You for exposing me to the need to deal with strongholds in my life and in my disposition. I ask You this week for a clearer understanding of the disposition You designed me for good and for doing Your will. Help me to see how sin has distorted my disposition and created strongholds in me that I can't destroy without Your help and power. As scary as it may be, give me a vision this week of the entrenched and towering strongholds in my life. Please remind me along the way that no argument, lofty opinion, or rebellious thought is beyond Your power to demolish. Do that good work in me, Lord. In Jesus' awesome name I pray, amen.

DAY 2
BATTLEFIELDS AND THINKING PATTERNS

Yesterday we mentioned how Rebekah went to the Lord and He told her the two nations within her were already exercising their dispositions. Fast forward to the end of her pregnancy: "When her days to give birth were completed, behold, there were twins in her womb. The first came out red, all his body like a hairy cloak, so they called his name Esau. Afterward his brother came out with his hand holding Esau's heel, so his name was called Jacob" (Gen.25:24-26).

Why did the newborn Jacob hang on to his brother's foot? Because he wanted to be born first. The name Jacob means heal catcher or heal grabber. It's the idea of wanting to find a way, even to deceive. It can mean to get ahead of the other. Do you see how their dispositions are already right there? God's Word is not saying, Oh! How interesting! How random! He was holding onto his heal. Isn't that cute and funny? No. The Bible is saying that what they will become was present in their delivery, in their prenatal character.

We first see clues about disposition in a child's behaviors. It doesn't take long before we begin to notice that he or she responds to the world in certain, often predictable, ways, related to his or her disposition.

MY DISPOSITION DICTATES MY THINKING PATTERN

You know I'm always looking for a way to get illustrations from my five grandsons. Two of our children and their spouses have given Kathy and me five unique and amazing little boys. Some of their distinctive traits can be seen in seconds; others require a few hours of observation, but each of them has clearly had his own disposition from birth.

Can we see the telltale signs of dispositions in ourselves? Can you see that you were born with a way of thinking that you have battled your whole life?

Can you see how your disposition has a lot to do with how you process what happens in your home, with your kids, in your marriage, in your finances, where you work, at your church?

Stop for a moment and review the paragraph you just read. Come up with three examples of how the way you think may be negatively affecting those around you.

Realize that if you just skipped over the little assignment above, you've revealed a stronghold in your disposition. The arguments, and the lofty opinions that keep you from reflecting on their possible existence, show that strongholds have taken up residence—in your disposition.

DISPOSITION AFFECTS MY PACE-THINKING

In Genesis 25:27 we learn more about Rebekah's sons: "When the boys grew up, Esau was a skillful hunter, a man of the field, while Jacob was a quiet man, dwelling in tents." We've jumped from birth to at least their late teen years. They are twins and yet could they be any more different? Esau is a hunter and tracker. He is well built and hairy. I picture him as muscular with a big red beard halfway down his chest. He's an outdoorsman.

We'll learn later that Jacob is the great indoorsman. He is super precise. He relies on his ability to read people. He is planning for the future. As we see in the text here, he's focused on the advantages that his brother seems oblivious to having.

Despite their obvious differences, Jacob is not more of a man than Esau, and Esau is not more of a man than Jacob. I hate this notion that manhood is a narrowly defined list of skills or likes and dislikes. It is wrong to think that being a man or even being Christ-like is like cloning. The assumption that all men should be the same, or that if Christians were like Jesus then they would all be the same, is nonsense.

What does it mean to be Christ-like if it isn't all of us becoming the same?

We all have our own dispositions. God loves the disposition that He has given to His men and His women. He is able to display the character of His Son through any disposition, but He is weary of seeing strongholds take advantage of what He created for good and to advance His own purposes. The goal of thinking differently is not to all think the same; the goal of thinking differently is to take every thought captive to the obedience of Christ and to destroy the strongholds of disposition, including the way that humans judge one another.

God's Word does not make a judgment between the dispositions of Jacob and Esau. If we read the entire account we find each brother had admirable qualities as well as shameful ones. They both had strongholds. I just want to dispense once and for all with the notion that masculinity (which is the subject here) has a singular expression. That idea wounds a lot of men. Let's be who God created us to be. Let's tear down the strongholds. Let's build up Christ-likeness in all of its expressions through His followers.

DISPOSITION AFFECTS PEOPLE-THINKING

In Genesis 25:28, the attention shifts to the twins parents, "Isaac loved Esau because he ate of his game, but Rebekah loved Jacob." How messed up is that? We're going to get into this home of origin strongholds next week, but I'll just say here that the situation is hugely messed up. Parents aren't supposed to have favorites! Isaac and Rebekah were themselves afflicted with strongholds.

How many kids are thrust into that through marital conflict and breakup? The kids feel torn and used like pawns. It's just awful.

How has your disposition created some challenges for you in dealing with other people?

DISPOSITION AFFECTS PASSION-THINKING

Read Genesis 25:29-34 in your Bible. Esau lived in the moment and didn't hesitate to be loud and demanding. Hebrews 12:15-17 tells us that Esau was a profane person. He was godless. With his birthright, Esau should have handled his inheritance with much more respect. Meanwhile, Jacob was taking full advantage of his brother, counting on Esau's appetites as a weakness he could exploit. Jacob had always resented the fact that his twin brother got a double portion when he was only born a few seconds earlier, so he used his savory stew to manipulate his profane brother who didn't respect his father's blessing. These two brothers had so many strongholds that affected what they were passionate about.

What provokes passion in you? Keep those things in mind as we review dispositions.

Your disposition even affects how you view the story of Jacob and Esau. Tomorrow we want to begin to talk about dispositions. I want you to be able to understand yourself.

Even if you're not sure about your disposition right now, take a moment to thank God for making you the way you are.

DISPOSITION REVIEW

The following chart summarizes the four basic dispositions that make up human personalities. Refer to it as you review the information we covered in the video lesson.

4 DISPOSITIONS

DISPOSITION	MAIN FOCUS	NEEDS	DOWNSIDE
Choleric			
Sanguine			
Phlegmatic			
Melancholy			

Choleric, Sanguine, Phlegmatic, and Melancholy are the four main temperaments. To help you figure out which one you are, let's just begin to go through them again as we did in the video lesson.

CHOLERIC

- The main focus of the choleric is the driver. They move. They set things in motion.
- The need of the choleric is that they need to win.
- The downside of the choleric personality is that they're frequently too aggressive.
- The choleric's view of time is now. If a choleric asks you to do something, he or she has never ever thought about when you would do it; it's always now.
- Choleric's view of authority is that "rulers rule!" They take charge—a way of looking at authority that is unique to cholerics.
- Choleric's people problem is that if they're not careful, they can use people. They can see people as a way to get their goal accomplished, as a means to an end, and not see them as people who should be treasured for who they are.

The apostle Paul is a good example of a choleric in the Bible. In terms of occupations, a lot of cholerics become CEOs. Hundreds of years ago, cholerics became explorers. Christopher Columbus was a choleric. What other kind of person would sail over the edge of the world?

Who do you know who is probably a choleric? How would you encourage someone with that disposition?

SANGUINE

- A sanguine, on the other hand, is expressive. Don't ever ask a sanguine what he or she thinks because you won't need to; they're already halfway into telling you.
- Sanguines are fun. They're the funniest people. Many sanguines are comedians.
- The downside of the sanguine is impulsiveness. While not aggressive like the choleric, they can become that way when they're in conflict.
- Sanguines view of time means they seldom wear watches. They don't need them. Sanguines are always late to the party. But when they get there, it's awesome—but you're never sure if they're going to make it. The reason why they're late to the party is because they were partying somewhere else. Parties don't start for the sanguine; they begin with eyes opening in the morning and end sometime after eyes closing at night.
- The sanguine sees authority as majority rule. It's more fun when everybody decides!
- The sanguine loves people, has a ton of relationships, and doesn't want to go forward without everyone on board. The sanguine grieves the loss of anyone. Sanguines are people-people to the max.
- The people problem of sanguines is that they are people pleasers. They can let people get away with things that aren't healthy. They try too hard to win people and get into compromises that aren't really right.

The apostle Peter was a sanguine. Sanguines make good entrepreneurs. While everyone else is trying to figure out if it's worth the risk, sanguines have already started. They are entertainers.

Who do you know who is probably a sanguine? How would you encourage someone with that disposition?

PHLEGMATIC

If you're the phlegmatic, you've been waiting patiently—somewhat indifferently—for me to get to you.

- Phlegmatics are actually amiable; they get along the best. They have the least conflict. They find a way. They don't buy into judgments in either direction—they're outside of the conflict.
- What phlegmatics need is to be safe. They're the ones trying to be peacemakers.
- The downside of phlegmatics is that they can be too passive. When something needs doing, it can take a lot of pressure on the phlegmatic to get it done.
- The phlegmatic sees time as tomorrow.
- The phlegmatic has everything perfectly ordered all of the time. The phlegmatic's car is always clean. And the thing that the sanguines do in their car would never be allowed in a phlegmatic's car—ever!
- If you ask a phlegmatic to plan a party, it's not going to go well. This is what you have to understand about phlegmatics—they're not like the choleric ("rulers rule!") or like the sanguine ("majority rules!"). They are on their own program and timetable.
- For the phlegmatic, "order rules." Whatever keeps the order—that's the rule. Is the phlegmatic's garage disorganized? It is not—or they can't sleep until it is. You can see what an immense strength and contribution these people bring to projects and organizations.
- Phlegmatics's people problem is that sometimes they may just feel that people aren't worth the effort. Unlike the extroverted temperaments of the choleric and the sanguine, they're not energized by people. When people become complicated, they withdraw. It's just not worth the effort. Phlegmatics don't have the same need for people.

Abraham's disposition was phlegmatic. Many doctors are phlegmatics, challenged to overcome sicknesses and fix bodies but not necessarily to manage people. That's why the subject of patient advocacy is such a big deal. If all of the doctors were choleric, you wouldn't need anyone else to insist on knowing what's going on, but Dr. Phlegmatic is just kind of laid back, super chilled, calm as circumstances unfold but not all that sensitive to the human side of the medical environment.

Who do you know who is probably a phlegmatic? How would you encourage someone with that disposition?

As with all of the temperaments, our filter is that we want to receive all of the benefits of people's dispositions but not understand that all of us have our downsides. The body of Christ is supposed to be the safest and most loving place to surface your downside because people who have been saved from their sins should know that we all have one. Yet, there is a common stronghold, the stubborn refusal to see this fact and wishing that "everyone could be the way we think that we are."

MELANCHOLY

- Melancholies are the analytics. That's their main focus. They have it totally analyzed.
- What melancholies need is precision or preciseness.
- The downside of melancholics is that they can get negative.
- The melancholy's view of time is punctual. If you have a melancholy in your marriage and you're not one, that can be an issue. We should be tearing down these strongholds and not seeing our own ways as superior.
- A melancholy's view of authority is not that "rulers rule," "majority rules," or that "order rules." For them, "rules rule." The melancholy keeps the speed limit carefully, one or two m.p.h. under in case the speedometer is not properly calibrated.
- Their people problem is that sometimes they despair of people and see people as even being beyond help.

Moses is an example of the melancholy disposition. Moses was feeling-oriented and very compassionate. A common career for a melancholy is an accountant. Melancholies have also often been artists such as Mozart and Van Gogh. Where would our world be without melancholies? They're the scientists. I mean we would be seriously up a creek without a paddle if the whole world was sanguine or choleric! These are often major talent contributing kinds of people.

Who do you know who is probably a melancholy? How would you encourage someone with that disposition?

Hopefully you are seeing traits in a couple of these dispositions that resonate with you. The stronghold of thinking that one disposition is better or more important than the others and your lofty opinions about the way that you are all have to be destroyed. Those strongholds have to be torn down. As Paul said, "The eye cannot say to the hand, 'I have no need of you,' nor again the head to the feet, 'I have no need of you' " (1 Cor. 12:21). All of us are needed.

DEMOLISHING DISPOSITION STRONGHOLDS

The following chart takes our study of dispositions to a deeper level, confronting some of the obvious strongholds that are often present in particular dispositions. Refer to this chart as you are reviewing the descriptions.

DESTROYING STRONGHOLDS

DISPOSITION	STRONGHOLD	ARGUMENT	LOFTY OPINION
CHOLERIC	Be successful	I have to win	I'm so effective
SANGUINE	Be popular	I have to make a splash	I'm so influential
PHLEGMATIC	Be consistent	I have to make peace	I'm so measured
MELANCHOLY	Be right	I have to be true to myself	I'm so honorable

CHOLERIC

The stronghold for the choleric is to be successful. The choleric thinks, *Whatever happens, I have to be a success. I have to get it done. I have to build the building. I have to meet the sales quota. I have to organize the team.* That is the driving force beyond the choleric.

The choleric's argument is the need to win. The Bible tells a choleric there's nothing wrong with winning as long as victory doesn't become the god he or she worships. Jesus said, "For what does it profit a man to gain the whole world and forfeit his soul?" (Mark 8:36). It turns out that winning at any cost costs you everything and isn't worth it.

According to 2 Corinthians 10:3-6, we're destroying strongholds and every argument and lofty opinion. The lofty opinion of the choleric is, "Look how much I got done. What are all of you people doing? If all of you people were only doing as much as I do." That prideful view can't see God may have others on a different timetable and pace.

SANGUINE

Of course, the stronghold of sanguines is to be popular and to be liked. That makes them great with people, but it can make them need people too much. Their argument is, "Well, I have to make a splash. I have to make an impact. People have to know I was here."

You always know when sanguines are there; they don't fail at that. But their lofty opinion is that they base their whole worth on being influential, not necessarily how they use the influence, just having it. They can also have a lofty opinion about themselves because of it.

They look at how many people are around them versus how many people are around you. Because of popularity they can fall into forming judgments wrong about themselves and wrong about you.

PHLEGMATIC

The stronghold of phlegmatics is a passion for consistency. They think they have to be consistent. They have to be the same every day.

And they are. I've worked with phlegmatics for years, and they are remarkably consistent and, therefore, dependable. That is an awesome strength, but if my wise phlegmatic friend were writing this I know that he would say his plodding uniformity has also been something that he has had to battle through. He thinks he can never get outside of the box. He resists even attempting spontaneity. A phlegmatic's sense of decorum is so governing to him that it can be restrictive to his usefulness at times.

Of course the argument he believes is, *I have to make peace. Everyone has to get along.* On some days that is so appreciated, but on other days, it's so unhelpful if it prevents necessary and healthy confrontation of problems.

The lofty opinion of phlegmatics is *I am so measured, under control.* They feel really good about that until it makes them look down on others who are responding in other ways.

Their lofty opinion could be that they are the most effective and influential people in the group.

MELANCHOLY

The stronghold of the melancholy is to be right. Don't get on the wrong side.

> *A brother offended is more unyielding than a strong city.*
> **PROVERBS 18:19**

A melancholy offended is very, very hard to win.

The argument that melancholies believe is *I have to be true to myself. How can I possibly work this out with you? I have to be true to myself.*

Of course, the Lord should be our highest loyalty, not ourselves. And their lofty opinion is *I am so honorable. Look at me how I've handled this. I've handled this right.*

The key to destroying the strongholds of disposition is taking every thought captive to the obedience of Christ.

> *...as Christ loved the church and gave himself up for her, that he might sanctify her, having cleansed her by the washing of water with the word.*
> **EPHESIANS 5:25-26**

Nothing will wash the stronghold of your disposition off your life than time spent washing your mind with the Word of God.

DAY 5
PERSONAL ENGAGEMENT

Last week we ended with the same title on day five. The final difficulty we looked at is the issue of personal engagement. We won't change unless we put ourselves on the line. Your temperament may or may not make this a big issue for you. Owning your own temperament is a risk because it makes you own your strengths while forcing you to consider your strongholds. But, without personal engagement, we will never think differently.

As you end this week, acknowledge that you are one of these dispositions: choleric, sanguine, phlegmatic, melancholy. If the last few days have felt like information overload, ask others to help you figure out the category of temperament that best fits you. Don't overlook the importance of asking God to help you pinpoint your disposition.

> **As a personal engagement decision, complete the following sentence with your temperament title: Lord, to the best of my understanding, I accept the fact that You designed me primarily with the disposition of a _____.**

But here is a second factor to consider: You're another temperament secondarily. These combinations of disposition greatly expand the way each of us is uniquely created. Your mix of dispositions can also make it a challenge to identify which is primary as well as differentiating what in each disposition are strengths and what are strongholds.

So, for example, I'm sanguine/choleric. I end up being more like a choleric at church because of all of my immense responsibility. That's one of the big tensions of my life. By disposition, I'm primarily sanguine, but by responsibility, I am pushed to emphasize my choleric tendencies. I've had to learn how crucial it is to surround myself with others who can keep me functioning in my strengths and avoid the strongholds that can so easily develop.

Alongside your primary temperament, what seems to be your likely secondary one?

Third, you cannot change—nor does God want you to change—your disposition. Passages such as Psalm 139:13-16 and Jeremiah 1:4-5 remind us how intimately God is involved in your design. He doesn't want to change how He has made you to be; He wants to demolish the strongholds that sin has built in you. As God made you, you are perfectly suited for what He wants you to do.

Take a moment to thank God for the way you are specifically related to your awareness of your temperament.

Fourth, because your unchangeable disposition must interact with countless other unchangeable dispositions, it's vital to account for your disposition in all your relationships. Love doesn't make the marriage; marriage makes the love. Marriage is the clearest example of a chosen commitment between two dispositions to live out life together. It doesn't take long to discover that you're married to a person who is so different than you. The context of marriage (or church or employment) brings you face-to-face with the sharp edges of your disposition and the need to reckon with other people that God has made different than you.

Under the instruction of 2 Corinthians 10:3-6, instead of entrenching our arguments and our lofty opinions, we are taking all those thoughts captive to the obedience of Christ. We are seeing God demolish strongholds. This means we are not affirming the husband who says, "This is the way I am, so you'll just have to accept it" as the final word. That unwillingness to account for both his own as well as his wife's temperament is so far out of bounds. Self-centered indulgence is not how to become like Jesus.

The wife pestering her husband to change is just as far out of bounds as he is. Both need to be seeking a godly, selfless, loving deference to one another. Pray about one another's strongholds , spouses; encourage one another's strengths. Marriages grow stronger as we passionately pursue a way to think differently.

How has your increased understanding of temperaments helped you recognize strengths and challenges in your relationships in a new way?

Fifth, the way you do something does not necessarily mean everyone else must do it the same way or be wrong. You may think counting is a one-and-done task until you watch an accountant do it. Then you might be thinking, *What on earth? Is he going to count again? He already knows what the total is.* Meanwhile, he's counting again. You may be convinced he's wasting his time

But wasting time is what it might mean if you were doing it; it doesn't mean the same if an accountant is doing it. Your irritation would be a sure sign you should never seek an accounting job! Instead, be deeply grateful that God actually wired some people to enjoy counting two or three times to make sure.

Whatever our own disposition, we should be thankful for the dispositions of others. Since there are four temperaments, if you're taking care of your 25 percent of what needs to be done, that means three other people are covering the 75 percent you can't do or would be driven crazy trying to do yourself. That discovery is a massive freedom. It also gives each of us excellent motivation to act on Romans 12:10, "Love one another with brotherly affection. Outdo one another in showing honor."

> **Make a list of at least three people whose dispositions are different than your own. Look for a way to express your gratitude to them for who they are and for the way their unique temperaments are a gift to you.**

> **Join me in this closing prayer:**
> *Lord Jesus, You've been given the name that is above every name. Our name is nothing. And our little viewpoint and my opinion—O God, would You tear down the strongholds in our dispositions? Would You wash our minds with Your Word? Would You forgive us for our harsh opinions and for our assessments of others.*
>
> *Lord, how it must grieve Your heart as we rail against those whom You love. We see the strongholds in others, but we don't see them in ourselves, God.*
>
> *Would You give us the grace to give to others? We have received so much grace. God, make us messengers of Your grace to others. Cause what we've learned this week not to fall heavily upon us but only heavily upon those strongholds, which keep us from expressing the way that You have created us to be. Please help us by Your Spirit. We pray in Jesus' name, amen.*

DESTROYING THE STRONGHOLDS OF FAMILY DYSFUNCTION (PART 1)

Welcome back to week 3 of Think Differently.

By this point, the phrase "nothing is different until you think differently" should be a fairly constant theme running in the back of your mind as you go about your days. Last week, we looked at demolishing the strongholds that we have in our dispositions, rooting out arguments and lofty opinions to bring our thinking into captivity to obey Christ. The next two weeks, we will confront an equally daunting battleground—the strongholds created by our family of origin.

Here's a fair warning: What you have learned about your disposition should help you understand some of the ways your family background has shaped you. As you consider the teaching this week and next, keep your disposition in mind. You may discover that some of the strongholds in your life are the result of your temperament coping with the home culture in which you grew up.

Use the following questions to open the discussion.

How have the last two weeks of teaching affected the way you think?

Now that you are aware of your disposition, what differences have you noticed this past week in your interactions with others?

Tell about one way in which your family background has shaped something you do almost every day.

To continue working on the memory Bible passage for this series, read together the following verses before watching the DVD segment:

> *For though we walk in the flesh, we are not waging war according to the flesh. For the weapons of our warfare are not of the flesh but have divine power to destroy strongholds. We destroy arguments and every lofty opinion raised against the knowledge of God, and take every thought captive to obey Christ, being ready to punish every disobedience, when your obedience is complete.*
> **2 CORINTHIANS 10:3-6**

WATCH

COMPLETE THE VIEWER GUIDE BELOW AS YOU WATCH DVD SESSION 3.

There are no _____ for generational sins, but there are
_____.

Some of the most obvious generational strongholds:

1. _____ _____

2. _____

3. _____

4. _____

5. _____

Exposing the bad decisions battles:

1. Where to _____—family vs. favorable?

2. Who to _____—attraction vs. character?

3. _____ group—easy vs. beneficial friendships?

4. _____ time—me vs. others?

5. Life _____—self vs. God?

DISCUSS THE DVD SEGMENT WITH YOUR GROUP, USING THE QUESTIONS BELOW.

Compared to the strongholds in our dispositions that we talked about last week, which seems like the bigger battle for you: temperament strongholds or family dysfunction strongholds? Why?

Besides the habitual lying that Abraham, Isaac, and Jacob illustrate as a generational sin, what other habits or behaviors might be generational sins?

Rather than blaming parents or previous generations for generational sins, what positive actions can we take when we recognize those strongholds in our lives?

In dealing with conflict resolution, would you say your family of origin was more fight, flight, or a mix? How about your present family (if you are married)?

James introduced the category of bad decision-making strongholds and offered five significant examples: where to live, who to marry, peer group choices, leisure time choices, and priorities. Which of these resonated with hard experiences in your life?

How did you respond to his indication of a preferred choice for each: family in living considerations, character in marriage choice, beneficial factors in peer associations, others as the focus of leisure, and the importance of godly priorities? Which would you like to discuss in greater depth?

Application: For each of the dysfunction strongholds in this lesson (generational sin, conflict resolution, and bad decision-making), try to identify at least one possible example in your own life. Ask the Lord to do what it will take to demolish those strongholds. Take a few minutes with the group to pray with each other asking for God's help in learning to think differently during these weeks.

This week's Scripture memory.

For the weapons of our warfare are not of the flesh but have divine power to destroy strongholds. **2 CORINTHIANS 10:4**

Assignment: Complete the daily lessons for this next week in preparation for the next group experience. Consider spending some time in the Book of Proverbs. Let those practical statements address some of your decision-making. Make a note of further questions or thoughts related to this week's teaching that you can share with other group members. Pray for each of your group by name, asking God to help them think differently this week.

The DVD session notes for this week included the memory verse that is part of the foundation passage for this entire series, 2 Corinthians 10:3-6. We are now looking at the strongholds that crowd our family history and create all kinds of dysfunctions. Second Corinthians 10:4-5 give us hope in the battlefield:

> *For the weapons of our warfare are not of the flesh but have divine power to destroy strongholds. We destroy arguments and every lofty opinion raised against the knowledge of God, and take every thought captive to obey Christ.*

Let me remind you that it is God's Word that renews our mind—the washing of the Word. By memorizing this Scripture, you'll already be heading in the right direction. When we memorize, we hide God's Word in our hearts. David said, "I have stored up your word in my heart, that I might not sin against you" (Ps. 119:11). When facing temptation (see Matt. 4:1-11), Jesus pulled out the sword of the Spirit (see Eph. 6:17) and used God's Word to destroy strongholds. When James says, "Resist the devil, and he will flee from you" (Jas. 4:7), the Word of God resists the enemy.

The battlefield tactic of taking every thought captive to obey Christ means we're choosing our thoughts. I don't have to let thoughts come into my head unbidden. I don't let my mind wander into wallowing over hurt, the past, and things that can't change. You and I can choose our thoughts. We can center our minds on the things of God and live in victory. It all comes down to what we think about.

I want to challenge you to memorize these verses—to hide them in your heart. Use them to demolish strongholds, the fortified places in your thinking. One place we can attack them is in our family dysfunctions.

RECON ON FAMILY DYSFUNCTION STRONGHOLDS

Today we want to begin some concentrated thinking about destroying the strongholds in our family of origin. It will take us two weeks to survey some of the most persistent ways in which dysfunctions create fixed patterns that become strongholds in our families. God's Word gives us an extended case study of a family, their strongholds included, that takes up much of the Book of Genesis. The parallels between how families worked back then and how they function now are practically identical. The settings and the cultural trappings may be different, but the human factors have remained unchanged. The functions and dysfunctions in families have been a constant since the first parents.

List at least three ways you benefited from your particular family of origin.

I realize that we're going into a sensitive subject here. Let me say at the outset that there is not going to be any parent bashing here. We're not looking at our past to find blame and let ourselves off the hook. The God-given capacity we use rightly or wrongly to assign blame is the very same capacity we use to own our responsibility, repent, and ask God for help. We want to understand our past so we see God's Word and His Spirit can demolish what seems set in stone.

The longer I'm a parent and the more decades I am away from my home of origin, the more grace I have for my parents and the more I recognize that they're people who are on a journey, too, to get free from some of the things with their parents. I just have faith to believe that the next generation will be better than my wife and I have been able to be. We just want to keep that going in the right direction. I know people have suffered in their home of origin. I know this is a sensitive subject.

What are some of the ways you intend for your family to be different from the family in which you were raised?

If we're going to think differently, we have to be willing to talk about the strongholds of family dysfunction. There are ways that you've been thinking for so long that you hardly even realize you're doing it, but it's the way your parents did or even what their parents did. We need to see those chains broken, so I'm going to try to wade in here where angels fear to tread, depending on God's wisdom and help every step of the way. I feel like Paul, writing to the Ephesians, when he said:

> For this reason I bow my knees before the Father, from whom every family in heaven and on earth is named, that according to the riches of his glory he may grant you to be strengthened with power through his Spirit in your inner being.
> **EPHESIANS 3:14-16**

With the Spirit's power we will see strongholds demolished and be strengthened to be all that God intended as individuals and families.

We have already defined strongholds as fortified ways of thinking that are resistant to change, but how are we using the term *dysfunction*? It's an important word because it names the problem while it affirms a basic truth. The prefix *dys*, meaning ill or bad, is used in combination with *function* to indicate something legitimate has gotten twisted or gone sideways. The family was designed by God with certain crucial functions Most mammals are born with a certain amount of survival equipment, like fur. We're born naked and totally dependent on our parents for our survival.

If you've never done it, consider expressing gratitude to your parents for giving you life. You are using that very important gift right now.

God also intended our homes to be the primary place where we would learn about Him. He gave the function of spiritual training to the family:

> And these words that I command you today shall be on your heart.
> You shall teach them diligently to your children, and shall talk of them

when you sit in your house, and when you walk by the way, and when
you lie down, and when you rise. You shall bind them as a sign on your
hand, and they shall be as frontlets between your eyes. You shall write
them on the doorposts of your house and on your gates.
DEUTERONOMY 6:6-9

These are commands to parents, a job description that shapes their relationship with their children and the atmosphere that should be present in the home. God wants the conversations at meals and during travel, in the evening and in the morning to have as their subject matter Him and His ways.

In what ways have you built into your home life occasions when God's Word and God's ways are discussed?

One of the areas of frequent surprise for young marrieds is finding out that not every family does things the way your family did it. And "it" isn't just some little thing here or there—it's almost everything!

What are some of the differences between the cultures of your family of origin and your spouse's? Which aspects (such as holiday traditions) have been challenges to harmonize?

As we look at family dysfunctions these next two weeks, it will be important to remember that differences do not automatically mean dysfunctions.

Healthy couples learn to harmonize their family of origin cultures, choosing a mix of good practices from the past and actively creating a life that is unique to them. They also work at encouraging one another to see the dysfunctions from their past demolished by the work of God's Spirit in each other's lives.

Pray for your spouse and your marriage this week, asking God to help you, practice grace in differences and to depend on God Spirit as you build a healthy family life together that honors Him.

GENERATIONAL SIN STRONGHOLDS

Please take a moment and read Genesis 26:1-11. There is a common dysfunction in families called generational sin. In order to understand Jacob better, we're going to look at Jacob's father Isaac.

Genesis 26:1 tells us there was a famine much like a previous famine in Abraham's time (see Gen. 12:10-20). This presents a similar set of events that both the father (Abraham) and the son (Isaac) had to deal with. Abraham responded to the famine by traveling to Egypt; God intervened and told Isaac to stay in Gerar, a Philistine royal city located in modern Palestine, in all likelihood because he was about to follow in his father's sandal tracks. But God wanted to impress on Isaac that His blessings were tied to the land: "Do not go down to Egypt; dwell in the land of which I shall tell you" (Gen. 26:2).

God then went on in verses 3-5 to reiterate His covenant with Abraham and his offspring, including the significant promise, "And in your offspring all the nations of the earth shall be blessed" (v. 4). Of course that's prophetic of Abraham's descendant Jesus Christ, the Messiah through whom all of us have been blessed.

> **How does God's covenant with Abraham and Isaac affect you?**
> **(If you're not sure, check out Galatians 3:7-9 and Romans 10:5-13**
> **to better understand why.)**

In Genesis 26:6-11, we can see a generational sin unfold right beside a generational obedience. First, there was generational obedience when Isaac married into his own extended family rather than choosing a wife from the pagan nations around him (see Gen. 24). Abraham preserved his family line by sending a servant to Haran to find a wife for his son. Eliezer returned with this woman (Rebekah) who was stunningly beautiful. Apparently lovely women ran in the clan. This also set up the circumstances for a generational sin.

"When the men of the place asked him about his wife, he said, 'She is my sister,' for he feared to say, 'My wife,' thinking, 'lest the men of the place should kill me because of Rebekah,' because she was attractive in appearance" (Gen. 26:7). Notice that the motivation behind his answer was fear.

It wasn't long before Abimelech the king noticed that Isaac and Rebekah weren't exactly treating each other as brother-sister but as marrieds. If you have a study Bible, the term *laughing* in verse 8 is the Hebrew word that suggests an intimate relationship. A strong confrontation follows: "So Abimelech called Isaac and said, 'Behold, she is your wife. How then could you say, "She is my sister"?' Isaac said to him, 'Because I thought, "Lest I die because of her"'" (v. 9).

Isaac's response is freaky, selfish, deceptive, and fearful. Isaac had a stronghold of fear. Here a pagan king showed greater sensitivity to the dangers of adultery than the child of God's promise. But God was also sovereignly stepping in to protect the heritage of the birth of Jesus Christ.

The underlying point here is that Isaac's lie was not invented in a vacuum. If we turn back to Genesis 12 and 20 we will observe Isaac's father Abraham using this same tactic twice: once in Egypt (12:11-20) and again in Gerar (20:1-18). In the latter case, Abraham was actually dealing with Abimelech, the father of the leader who confronted Isaac. A pattern of sin in one generation can lead to generational sin in the next generations.

Abraham's (phlegmatic) primary issue was fear and trust. Isaac (phlegmatic) struggled with the exact same sin as his father. When the pressure was on and a threat was present, both Abraham and Isaac made decisions out of fear. Cover up! Hide! Lie about the truth!

By the time you see this in the third generation, the chains are strong in Jacob, who is not even phlegmatic. Lying has become so engrained that it is the default practice: deception to avoid pain, deceit to advance pleasure, or cheating for no reason. If we had asked Jacob, "Why do you lie so much?" he would likely have answered, "It's what I DO. It's what I ALWAYS do. It was in my family. My dad was a liar. My grandpa was a liar. We lie."

When we lie to avoid pressure on us, that may be generational sin. When we echo a sinful attitude or action that we witnessed in our parents or grandparents, we are propagating generational sin, though we may not immediately recognize it as part of our heritage. One of the eerie experiences in confronting sin in our lives and our families is that some generational sins may go back many generations. Each new generation either reinforces the stronghold or finally let's God demolish it. If a stronghold is left intact, it will likely be inherited by the next generation. The desire to destroy a family dysfunction is much more than the significant improvement of our own lives; it also involves what future generations will have to confront.

Tomorrow we will review a number of common generational sins. As a result of the video or these last few pages, what practices are you now aware of that might be generational sins in your family? It may be time to ask God to demolish them.

Let me add an important note about generational sin. Deuteronomy 24:16 tells us, "Fathers shall not be put to death because of their children, nor shall children be put to death because of their fathers. Each one shall be put to death for his own sin." That means no matter what your kids do, God will not punish you for their choices. And kids, (even adult kids), God won't punish you for your parents sins.

How does that square with generational sin? Deuteronomy 5:9-10 also points out that God is involved in "visiting the iniquity of the fathers on the children to the third and fourth generation of those who hate me." Does God, then, withhold punishment from or visit iniquity upon one generation because of the actions of a previous generation? The answer is both! God does not judge us because of how your father, mother, grandfathers, or grandmothers struggled. Because of sin in your family's past, you can have certain temptations, inclinations, and vulnerabilities. If we're going to think differently and live in godly ways, we have to do some identifying and demolishing of those generational sin strongholds.

In this battle we find a statement of hope in the words of 1 John 4:4, "He who is in you is greater than he who is in the world." God's power is more than sufficient for this battle. But if we're going to think differently, then we're going to be aware and trust God.

DAY 3

A CATALOG OF GENERATIONAL SINS

Before we look at five common generational sins, let me remind you of a crucial dynamic that was part of Abraham's experience and is part of yours. Genesis 20:1-2 sets up the scene: "From there Abraham journeyed toward the territory of the Negeb and lived between Kadesh and Shur; and he sojourned in Gerar. And Abraham said of Sarah his wife, 'She is my sister.' And Abimelech king of Gerar sent and took Sarah." He lied about his wife Sarah to Abimelech, but the tactic had unintended consequences. Abraham was left alive, but he suddenly lost his wife. Abimelech reasonably concluded, "If she's not your wife, I'll make her one of mine!"

The next verse begins with the words, "But God" (v. 3). There was another interested party involved in Abraham's life. God's plan to create a people for Himself was in play. The heritage of Jesus Christ was at risk. And God made a move. The same is true of your life. How many things in our lives hinge on those two words: "But God"?

The testimony of every believer is some form of this statement: *I was thinking, planning, going _____, but God intervened. God dropped a boulder of reality on my false world and showed me my condition*. When God breaks into our lives, that's grace right there.

How does the phrase "But God" fit in describing your experience in recognizing that you need a savior?

When recently has God sovereignly interrupted your plans or actions to get you back on track with His plans?

What are some of the strongholds that can be passed on from one generation to another? Here are some generational stronghold categories:

SUBSTANCE ABUSE

Multiple generations in a family can be hounded by certain false escapes. They turn to alcohol; they don't turn to God. They turn to smoking pot and other kinds of medications that inebriate the ability to feel pain. And because it blocks the pain, it blocks the God-given prod to get us to a better place.

Take a mental survey of your medicine cabinet and hiding places. What substances could serve or are serving as a ready alternative to seeking God's help for challenges in life?

Are there known abuses from previous generations that you have avoided by substituting other abuses? (One generation's struggle with alcohol can easily show up in the next generation as some other kind of abuse.)

MATERIALISM

Maybe you grew up in a family where everything was about the next thing. Does this sound familiar? "We're going to get one of these. We're going to buy, own it, polish it, and enjoy it. This is our life! Our stuff! You better not TOUCH my boat! WHO SCRATCHED MY BOAT?!"

If you grew up with, "My stuff! My stuff! My stuff!," that can become a real stronghold for people. As I often say, it's not wrong to have a thing, but if that thing has you, that's a threat to God. And it will be taken out. It's much better to have that stronghold broken.

How do you tell the difference between something you own and something that owns you?

Ask God to show you possessions that have become idols in your life.

GLUTTONY AND OTHER FOOD DISORDERS

Maybe you grew up in a home where the amount of food that was served at the table was three times what was needed, and you had someone whose identity was tied up in seeing you enjoy food. So everyone in your family has battled obesity because food had a place that it wasn't supposed to have. Perhaps bulimia has been a byproduct for some. Food can indicate a stronghold.

How are the current eating habits in your family a reflection and/or resistance to the food traditions in previous generations?

LUST

Pornography and other sexual perversions, even when apparently kept hidden, show up in succeeding generations. Sadly, sexual abusers may have grown up the children of sexual abusers. These strongholds require God's intervention in a big way.

The rampant exposure to porn on the Internet may be making you the generation that initiates or escalates this destructive pattern. How do you maintain accountability over the sexual area of your life?

SELFISHNESS

Do you find yourself echoing these thoughts you've heard all your life? "We only do what's best for us. Just the people at this house. We don't serve anyone. We don't give ourselves to anyone." Selfishness can become a generational sin and stronghold.

What's the difference between healthy family solidarity and family selfishness?

When would choosing to do without as a family actually be a beneficial practice?

This isn't an easy list to apply personally. Some of these items may hit close to home, but we need to speak truth to one another in love if we are destroying the strongholds in family dysfunction.

Pray about generational sins in your family. Do some journaling about your family history. If your parents/grandparents are living, gently ask them about patterns you suspect. Lift up your parents and grandparents in prayer.

We ended yesterday with words of hope about generational sins. Here are some more. Back to Deuteronomy 5:9-10 where God is warning He is "visiting the iniquity of the fathers on the children to the third and fourth generation of those who hate me" (v. 9). This is where you stop and say, "But I don't hate God!" I'm glad to hear that because God immediately goes on to say, "but showing steadfast love to thousands of those who love me and keep my commandments" (v. 10).

God draws near to those who want to follow and obey Him. He is pleased with those who honor Him. He stands with those who want to break the chains of generational sins in their family.

Make this your prayer:
Lord, I want to do everything I can as long I'm drawing breath to make sure I get victory over some things so that my kids don't struggle with the things that I struggle with, and so my grandkids—when I'm off of this earth—are not battling things that I wouldn't let God get me victory over. Help me, Lord. In Jesus' name, amen.

DAY 4

STRONGHOLDS AND CONFLICT RESOLUTION

In discussing our dispositions last week, there were two broad categories we didn't mention that affect all the temperaments. Some of us are extroverts and some of us are introverts. Extroverts tend to be others-oriented; introverts tend to be the opposite, inner-oriented. Extroverts tend toward fight; introverts tend toward flight.

Because we are looking at family of origin issues, it's often helpful to identify the general characteristics of our home life. Some of us grew up in a "fight" home with extroverted parents, others in a "flight" home with introverted parents, but the reality is that many of us probably grew up in a home with one of each. We had a mother or a father who would fight it out while the opposite spouse was always trying to smooth things over, hope for the best, or deal with it later. How conflict was dealt with can become a massive stronghold in the lives of God's people. We want that destroyed.

> **Describe your childhood home life using the fight/flight or shouting/ silence language to identify the level of introverted and extroverted tendencies from your parents.**

Read Genesis 26:12-22. Isaac was not living where God wanted him to live; he was living in Gerar with the Philistine nation. The Philistines became a problem for Israel up through the life of David and beyond, but God's blessing on Isaac's life resulted in him becoming very wealthy and provoking the envy of the Philistines. They expressed this envy by filling in wells that Abraham had dug and claiming the new wells Isaac's servants dug. These hostile actions endangered Isaac's flocks.

> **Imagine if your dad had dug all of these wells in the land that God gave him. You're the bigger and more powerful person, but your enemies who have already told you that they're afraid of you come and start filling in your wells. How would you respond?**

Well, this is what Isaac did. "So Isaac departed from there" (v. 17). Isaac's flight response caused him to say, "You want me to leave? I'll leave. Where do you want me to go? Tell me where you want me to go and I'll go there." Three different wells were re-dug by Isaac's men before the quarreling ran its course. At that point, Isaac had moved to Beersheba (v. 23) which place him back in the promised land.

What conclusions might we draw from Isaac's actions? The point here isn't that Isaac was wrong in every instance to avoid the conflict, rather that Isaac's wrongness is in the fact that avoidance is all he did. He just ran from conflict. His stronghold was based in fear. Phlegmatics fear. And so Isaac made his decisions based upon that stronghold.

Sometimes flight is the right thing, but sometimes engagement and even a fight is right. Do we have to have some conflict? Let's have it, but let's have it in a healthy way. Depending on the circumstances, either response should be on the table.

> **How does your temperament tend to respond to conflict (especially if you are not a phlegmatic)?**

> **Under pressure, do you believe it's better to have a consistent response or to have a consistent pattern of considering the circumstances before responding? Why?**

If you want to know what God thinks about Isaac's motivation, note what God told him in Genesis 26:24, "And the LORD appeared to him the same night and said, 'I am the God of Abraham your father. Fear not.'" This is God's Word to all of us. Second Timothy 1:7 reminds us that "God gave us a spirit not of fear but of power and love and self-control." God doesn't want His children living in fear, yet fear is a huge stronghold for many.

My point here is whatever is your way of dealing with conflict, the stronghold of fear is the "one-size-fits-all" approach to conflict resolution. The problem is that we always want to do what we do naturally and easily. Consistency in conflict resolution is no more a wise tactic than assuming that in a conflict that you're always right. Several factors determine the wise way to respond in a conflict situation:

- What if the other person isn't ready?

- What if it's better left alone for now?

- What if you need more time to see your own role or fault in the problem?

- What if waiting, praying, learning, and loving sets the stage for a better resolution down the road?

It's true on the other side too. Maybe you were taught to never fight, but if your default response to conflict is to flee, here are some questions to answer to help you respond:

- What if inaction causes greater danger?

- What if doing nothing, leaving it alone, makes it worse?

- What if doing nothing communicates you don't care?

- What if someone is doing the same thing to other people that they did to you?

What help did you find in the two lists of questions above for handling the conflicts in your life?

What I'm trying to make clear is that there is no "one-size-fits-all" in responding to pressure. The stronghold is not being present in the moment with the God who says, "Fear not," and wisely discerning what is needed today in that situation. The need may change from day to day. We can walk with God today and trust Him for the wisdom to think differently and to do what the situation warrants that represents His heart to love and to advance His purposes for reconciliation.

Ask God to help you remember in conflict that your instinctive temperament-based response may not be the best in that situation. Give Him permission to train you to respond under His guidance in any situation.

BAD DECISION-MAKING STRONGHOLDS

At this point you may be saying to yourself, *Well, my problem isn't the generational stuff and it isn't conflict resolution. My problem is that my family just never really worked very well. My home of origin always seemed out of sync. We didn't ever get the bills paid. There were job changes all of the time. We kept moving and relocating. Our family could never seem to get traction out of the mud of life. We never got on the main road. It was just one problem after another.*

If this family history is familiar to you, realize that it points to a stronghold of bad decision-making. Your parents just made bad decisions. You may be following their example and also making poor choices.

> **If you don't know Proverbs 3:5-6 by heart, look it up. How do these two verses compare with your normal decision-making process?**

Unfortunately, your experience is not that uncommon. There are plenty of examples in God's Word. Continuing with Jacob's story, let's look briefly at his brother Esau. Genesis 26:34-35 says, "When Esau was forty years old, he took Judith the daughter of Beeri the Hittite to be his wife, and Basemath the daughter of Elon the Hittite, and they made life bitter for Isaac and Rebekah." First, it's interesting to note that Esau married at the same age his dad was when Rebekah arrived as Isaac's wife (see Genesis 25:20). Dads do influence their children. At least Abraham made the arrangements for Isaac's marriage; it appears Isaac was too fearful of conflict to urge either of his sons toward marriage, even though everyone in the family knew about God's promise to build a nation.

Second, choosing on his own made it highly likely that Esau would make a bad decision. The Hittites were renowned pagan troublemakers. Esau brought not one but two godless women into the family. Now he wasn't emulating his father but his grandfather Abraham who had multiple wives.

So Esau married these two women. That word *bitter* in Genesis 26:35 literally means grief of mind. These two women were such a grief to Isaac's family that they were tormented by the misery caused by Esau's godless wives. If you think it went away quickly, look at Genesis 27:46 where Rebekah says to Isaac: "I loathe my life because of the Hittite women. If Jacob marries one of the Hittite women like these, one of the women of the land, what good will my life be to me?"

Rebekah had a stronghold of bitterness to deal with. Don't let your kids take the place of God in your life. Is your life all about your unmarried kids? We can't control their choices anyway! Raising kids isn't like baking cookies. There is no recipe. I've seen godly parents heartbroken by evil choices of rebellious children. I've seen kids brought up in horrific homes that broke through those barriers to serve God.

People make their choices. You can't do anything to guarantee your kids will follow the Lord. You can do some things to guarantee that they won't, and you never want to elevate your kids to the level of really becoming a stronghold in your life.

Many choices can't be reversed. Bad decisions can't be undone. But you don't have to continue making poor choices. Based on what you've learned so far, what needs to change in your decision-making process?

As you end this week's studies, take a few minutes to pray for the rest of your small group. Ask God to work powerfully in their lives to demolish strongholds.

WEEK 4

DESTROYING THE STRONGHOLDS OF FAMILY DYSFUNCTION (PART 2)

Welcome to week 4 of this group discussion of Think Differently.

This session we are continuing to study the Old Testament patriarch Jacob and his extended family to understand better the strongholds of family dysfunctions and why they must be demolished. It is true in our family life as much as in personal life that nothing is different until we think differently. May God help us get to that place where we really have changed our minds about the matters He cares about for us. Use the following questions to expand the discussion while encouraging everyone to participate.

In what ways did part one of this lesson help you appreciate your family of origin?

What was a significant new insight about family dysfunctions that came as a result of last week's session and studies?

Hopefully, you are developing a constant awareness that our thinking influences everything we do. One of the ways family dysfunctions function as strongholds is that they become established in us before we're even aware of them. We learn them as we're learning to walk. Along with all the good and practical lessons we learn within our families are also ways of thinking that can cripple us in many ways. It's time for thinking renewal.

Which of the three stronghold areas we looked at last week do you see as the most influential in your life: generational sin, conflict resolution, or bad decision-making? Why?

To prepare for this session and work together on the key memory passage for the entire series, read together the following verses:

> *For though we walk in the flesh, we are not waging war according to the flesh. For the weapons of our warfare are not of the flesh but have divine power to destroy strongholds. We destroy arguments and every lofty opinion raised against the knowledge of God, and take every thought captive to obey Christ, being ready to punish every disobedience, when your obedience is complete.*
> **2 CORINTHIANS 10:3-6**

WATCH

COMPLETE THE VIEWER GUIDE BELOW AS YOU WATCH DVD SESSION 4.

Mind in Scripture can mean everything from _____
to _____.

The problem is that we can't change our _____ — can't _____
differently—and can't destroy these strongholds until we know what they are.

Family of origin strongholds from last week:

1. _____ _____ strongholds

2. _____ _____ strongholds

3. Bad _____-_____ strongholds

Two more this week:

4. _____ _____ strongholds

5. _____ matters most strongholds

As James describes the strongholds, add notes in the margins about how what he
says relates to your particular temperament and strongholds.

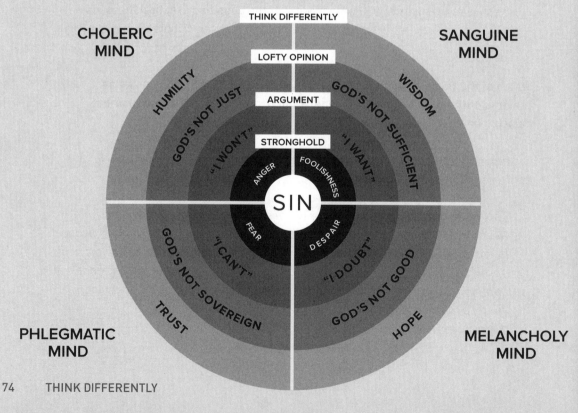

DISCUSS THE DVD SEGMENT WITH YOUR GROUP, USING THE QUESTIONS BELOW.

What is our group's make up when it comes to the primary temperaments? Who are the cholerics? Sanguines? Phlegmatics? Melancholies?

Now, what is each of you sensing is your secondary temperament?

How does this help you understand the rest of the group better? How can the rest of us confirm and encourage each of our temperaments?

In what ways has knowing your temperament started affecting the way you think and respond to situations and to other people?

How have you experienced God's help in becoming aware of strongholds and seeing strongholds start to crumble in your life?

In continuing his teaching on various family strongholds, James added two to the ones we learned about last week: selfish deception strongholds and money matters most strongholds. What examples of these two strongholds can you see in your family?

Based on the chart James used to explain the prevalent strongholds, arguments, and lofty opinions, share your thoughts in the following application exercise.

Application: Which stronghold, argument, or lofty opinion do you need to ask God to demolish in your life? Tell the group and ask them to pray for you. Take a few minutes with the group to pray with each other, asking for God's help in dealing with family strongholds when others aren't aware of them or interested in seeing them demolished.

This week's Scripture memory:

> *Submit yourselves therefore to God. Resist the devil, and he will flee from you.* **JAMES 4:7**

Assignment: Complete the daily lessons for this next week in preparation for the next group experience. Be intentional in noting strongholds as God reveals them to you. Pray for each of your group by name, asking God to help all of them think differently this week.

Thinking and thinking differently are the tasks of the mind. It's important to understand how God works in your mind and with your mind. Remember that according to Jesus, one aspect of the greatest commandment is to love God with our whole mind (see Mark 12:30).

The word *mind* in Scripture can mean everything from determination to memory. More than two hundred references in the Bible are about your mind. And we're discovering why—because nothing is different until we think differently. God is exceedingly interested in our minds. In fact, while we tend to think of following Jesus and imitating Jesus as a pretty physical thing, Philippians 2:5 reminds us it really begins, as all godliness beings, with our thinking: "Have this mind among yourselves, which is yours in Christ Jesus."

God is so interested in our minds that David noted, God knows "my thoughts from afar" (Ps. 139:2). When David says that God knows your thoughts, my thoughts, and our thoughts from afar off, what David is saying is, "I'm here. My thoughts are far off. I haven't even chosen those thoughts yet, but God already knows."

In fact, isn't it awesome to think that God knows how our thinking is going to be changed by these hours in His Word thinking about thinking differently? God already knows the impact that will be made in our mental, emotional, spiritual, and relational health. God already understands how you are going to respond to this message and how you're going to be changed by it. This is how important our thoughts are.

May God guide you as you apply your mind to the assignments each day this week.

WHAT DID WE LEARN LAST WEEK?

We have strongholds in our thinking. We've got fortified places in our minds that are resistant, stubbornly so, to God's Word and to God's will. Some of those stubborn patterns of thinking are from our disposition. We were born that way. But some of those strongholds come from our homes of origin. You may hardly know how much these family strongholds affect your thinking and choices, but they play a part in your life every day.

The problem is that until we know what they are we can't change our minds, think differently, and destroy these strongholds. That's why we talked about the disposition related strongholds as well as the strongholds related to our home of origin.

Here again are the three family strongholds we studied last time:

1. GENERATIONAL SIN STRONGHOLDS (GEN. 26:6-11).

Genesis 11–50 features the family tree of Abraham, beginning with his father, Terah and concluding in chapter 50 with the death of grandson, Jacob, and his great grandson, Joseph. Along the way we see the generational sin strongholds that dogged the family. One obvious problem was the use of lying that we see in Abraham and echoed in both his son Isaac and his grandson Jacob.

We learned in Deuteronomy 5:9 and Deuteronomy 24:16 that although God doesn't punish sons, grandsons, daughters, or granddaughters for their parents' or grandparents' sins, He does visit or affect "the iniquity of the fathers on the children to the third and fourth generation of those who hate me" (Deut. 5:9).

Some of those around us who are overwhelmed by problems may not just be making poor choices; they may be struggling against generations of accumulated habits. This ought to make us cautious in judgment of them. Your friend who keeps falling? Maybe she's not like you. She has her own disposition. She has her own home of origin. She has her own family line. Maybe things are harder for her than they are for you. God forgive us for our judgment of one another. God give us graciousness and a kindness, especially with people who are first generation believers trying to figure this all out.

> **Do a quick review of your circle on influence. If you know people who are clearly struggling with generational sins, encourage them. Maybe even invite them to be part of this group, or go through the series with them later.**

Be reminded that Deuteronomy 5:10 says that while God does visit the iniquities of the fathers upon the children to the fourth generation, He is also the God faithfully "showing steadfast love to thousands of those who love me and keep my commandments." These chains can be broken. Generational thinking can change. You can leave a godly heritage to those who come after you.

> **Take a worship break and thank God for His steadfast love to you and through you to your children and perhaps grandchildren.**

2. CONFLICT RESOLUTION STRONGHOLDS (GEN. 26:12-25).

Did you figure out what you learned from your parents about conflict resolution— fight or flight? We concluded last week, because opposites attract, that you probably had one of each in your home. The big problem isn't when the fighter is fighting; the big problem is when the flighter starts fighting. They hardly ever do that.

I don't know what was going on in your home of origin. Maybe there were some raised voices, some things broken, and even some physical contact. There are people in our church who frequently had the police at their house while growing up. My wife Kathy had that. By God's grace, we have never had that, but maybe you have. The point is to break the pattern. It's time to get that stronghold demolished.

We talked about Isaac's conflict resolution strongholds that made avoidance his only tactic. The problem isn't avoiding conflict because that is sometimes exactly what we need to do; the problem is that we always want to do it the way we do it.

Some of us never engage and some of us never walk away. That is the stronghold to be destroyed.

> **Some families who appear to be perfect are actually a massive mess of problems. It's the nature of family to insist on loyalty, and acknowledging dysfunctions feels like a betrayal when in actuality, blowing the whistle on a stronghold often sets everybody free. As you have prayerfully considered your family of origin, what issues has God shown you that might indicate a stronghold?**

> **What are you going to do about it?**

3. BAD DECISION-MAKING STRONGHOLDS (GEN. 26:34-35; 27:46).

As long as we insist on thinking the way we've always thought we're going to continue making decisions the way we always have and getting the same disappointing results. That's the power of entrenched ways of thinking in a family. A pattern of bad decisions is a sure clue that there are strongholds of wrong thinking in the background.

It's worth pausing for a caution to say that all disappointing outcomes don't necessarily mean a wrong decision was made. Sometimes we make all the right moves and things don't turn out as expected. Deciding to follow Jesus every day (one of the best decisions you could ever make) doesn't mean everything will be great all the time. The point is learning to spot strongholds in the way we make decisions.

In our family case study of Abraham's descendants, Esau married badly, but that was just the tip of the iceberg in this family because they were full of so much dysfunction from awful decision-making. The passivity of his father Isaac, the favoritism both Isaac and Rebekah practiced toward their sons, and the bitterness of Rebekah over Esau's choices were all evidences of underlying strongholds that were never demolished.

> **How would you summarize the two or three most important guidelines you use in making decisions?**

DAY 2
SELFISH DECEPTION STRONGHOLDS

This fourth category of family dysfunction points to the internal destructiveness within a family when each member is pursuing selfish purposes at the expense of other family members. When we look at the complex web of relationships between Isaac, Rebekah, Jacob, and Esau it isn't difficult to identify multiple cases of selfish deception in play at any one time. Each of these people had an agenda, and they pursued it without regard for the rest of the family.

Genesis 27 begins some time after Isaac and Rebekah's grief over Esau's marriage to two pagan women (Gen. 26:34-45). Isaac has aged to the point of losing his sight. When he realized he wasn't getting any younger, Isaac decided it was time to pass on the blessing to his eldest son:

> He said, "Behold, I am old; I do not know the day of my death. Now then, take your weapons, your quiver and your bow, and go out to the field and hunt game for me, and prepare for me delicious food, such as I love, and bring it to me so that I may eat, that my soul may bless you before I die."
> **GENESIS 27:2-4**

Isaac told Esau it was time to transfer spiritual and material prosperity from the father to the firstborn son. This was not a lighthearted "Bless you!" after a sneeze. The birthright (which Esau had already sold cheap to Jacob) and the blessing were tied up together. Just think wedding, dedication, baptism, graduation, and inheritance all tied into one event.

Generally speaking, when the event is in your honor, you're not involved, but what we're seeing here is that Isaac is exceedingly selfish. He was saying, I'll give you the blessing, but before I do, I have a special request. I'm old. I'm down to the wire here. Since I have to give this stuff somebody, I'll give it to you. But you do something for me first.

Read Genesis 27:5-45. Consider how each family member is causing harm to themselves and to others by what they do.

What evidence of selfishness strongholds do you see in your family? How specifically do you participate in those ways of treating others?

Isaac's selfish approach to the blessing set the stage for what followed. Isn't it amazing to see how Rebekah (ever the eavesdropper, ever the schemer) manipulated the three men in her family? She made use of privileged information to betray her son Esau and benefit her son Jacob. She deliberately twisted her husband's intentions for her own purposes. She overrode Jacob's fear over the plan to trick his father. Although Jacob was the player in deceiving his father with the substitute meal and clever outfit, it was Rebekah behind the scenes pulling the puppet strings. She devised the elaborate scheme to secure her husband's blessing on her favored son. And when she found out Esau wasn't going to take this disappointment without retribution, she immediately set a plan in motion to get Jacob out of harm's way by emotionally manipulating her husband again.

Jacob was not an innocent bystander in this elaborate dance of deception. He willingly, though fearfully, participated in his mother's scheme. He helped fine tune his mother's plan by raising the problem that Isaac's poor sight didn't affect his sense of touch or his sense of smell. Once he got into character, Jacob played his part like a consummate actor. He was rightly fearful that failure to perform might cause his father to curse him, but he immediately accepted his mother's willingness to accept the curse in his place. He had already tricked his brother into selling his birthright cheap; why not go for the father's blessing too? Jacob didn't even hesitate to implicate God in his deception. When it looked like Isaac might suspect something, Jacob had a ready answer: "But Isaac said to his son, 'How is it that you have found it so quickly, my son?' He answered, 'Because the LORD your God granted me success'" (Gen. 27:20). And he sealed the deal with a direct lie.

Meanwhile, Esau was living the self-centered, careless life of Isaac's favorite son. He realized he would occasionally have to reciprocate to his father for the special status beyond being the firstborn. Going out to shoot some wild game for dad was no big deal. If that's all it took to get the blessing from his aging father, he'd do it.

His other side erupted in bitterness when he realized he'd been duped again by that slightly younger, meddling brother! He pleaded with his father for some leftover blessing. His father's words were a grim reminder that Esau would live in rebellion toward his brother. And that began almost immediately when Esau announced plans that he would kill Jacob as soon as Isaac was dead.

In Genesis 27:27-29, Isaac blessed Jacob with words he had intended to use for Esau. His blessing is an amazing confirmation of the prophecy Rebekah was given before the boys were born (Gen. 25:23), except for the fact that the whole thing was pulled off with a massive lie. Did the outcome mess up God's plans? No. God worked within and despite the dysfunctions in Isaac and Rebekah's marriage to bring about His will, just like He does in all circumstances. But it remains true that dysfunctions were a massive stronghold in the family of Abraham. From the grandfather to the father to the son—it had to be broken.

You may be one who grew up in a home remarkably similar to Isaac's. It may have been a way of life to say, "We lie to get what we have to have. We deceive. And maybe it's not an outright lie—a bold-faced lie—but we steer it and spin it and twist it and find a way to get our way." You may still feel trapped in a web of family relationships that forms an unbreakable stronghold. You've been conditioned by experiences and time to think there's no way out, but that stronghold with its fiercely independent arguments and lofty opinions is not more powerful than God. That's why at the heart of all we're learning is the principle that things aren't going to be different until we think differently. We cannot think differently until our hearts and minds are under the direction of God and His Word.

As you end this day's homework, prayerfully read our core Bible text again. Apply it to your family situation and ask God to continue to do His work of demolishing strongholds and training you to think differently.

For though we walk in the flesh, we are not waging war according to the flesh. For the weapons of our warfare are not of the flesh but have divine power to destroy strongholds. We destroy arguments and every lofty opinion raised against the knowledge of God, and take every thought captive to obey Christ, being ready to punish every disobedience, when your obedience is complete.
2 CORINTHIANS 10:3-6

IDENTIFYING DECEPTION STRONGHOLDS

We looked at the complex and damaging effects of a fortified stronghold of deception in the family of Isaac and Rebekah. Each member of the family had certain assumptions about living that guided their deceptive actions. These were not necessarily conscious, deliberate thought patterns but established ways of relating to others that were not questioned. I've listed five here that we see in the account found in Genesis 27. They illustrate the defenses that a stronghold builds in people's lives to prevent them from thinking differently.

1. "MY NEEDS BEFORE YOUR NEEDS."

Isaac, Rebekah, Esau, and Jacob all treated one another with this standard operating deception. Isaac had the responsibility of speaking a blessing in his sons' lives, but he twisted it with favoritism and insisting on having a special meal to satisfy a personal craving. Rebekah had a view of her role as wife and mother that overrode all other considerations. She was willing to manipulate her husband and both her sons to maintain that role. Esau's version was, "My needs come first; I don't even recognize that you have needs." Jacob willingly colluded with his mother's plans to deceive his father and brother because his need to grasp came first. My need before your need is a selfish deception.

> **How does this self-deception fit with the Scripture, "Do nothing from selfish ambition or conceit, but in humility count others more significant than yourselves. Let each of you look not only to his own interests, but also to the interests of others" (Phil. 2:3-4)?**

2. "LYING IS BETTER THAN LOSING."

We don't see this problem so much in Esau, but his dad, mom, and brother had plenty to go around. Isaac had a history of lying. Rebekah faced a truth like the physical differences of her sons and created a deception to hide that truth from her husband. Jacob handled the prospect of losing out on the blessing by boldly lying to his dad.

> **Children raised in an atmosphere of lying and who never have their personal sinful inclination to lie challenged and corrected early on certainly grow up with this assumption in their relationships. How easy do you find it to lie and what do you do when you realize you've just lied?**

3. "UNDER PRESSURE, KEEP LYING."

Isaac wasn't sure he was dealing with Esau and gave Jacob several chances to tell the truth, but Jacob stuck to the deceptive script. His fear of his father's curse kicked in and spurred him to keep lying. When Rebekah's deception caused one of her sons to express the intent to kill her other son, she didn't hesitate to deceive her husband again.

One of the sure evidences that we are thinking differently comes when we stop lying and immediately repent when a lie is exposed.

> **One of the hard and healthy prayers we can make is to ask God to convict us of lies, compel us to repent, and confess to those to whom we have lied. How has God's Spirit been speaking to you about the matter of deception as a stronghold in your life?**

4. "WE PLAY THE CRAZY 'THIS IS MY FAVORITE KID' GAMES."

Isaac and Rebekah were a poster couple for dysfunctional parenting, illustrated by their practice of favoritism toward their children. We can see generational seeds of this dysfunction in Abraham and Sarah's treatment of their only son, Isaac, and the deceptive practices of Laban, Rebekah's brother, in dealing with Jacob later. Note how this was repeated in Jacob's life when he practiced the same kind of preferential parenting toward his son Joseph that created such trouble. They could have been treated individually rather than each becoming one parent's favorite and spurring an unhealthy competition between the sons.

If you are a parent, how are you going about loving each of your children in way that makes them feel special without making them feel like they are more special than their siblings?

5. "IF IN DOUBT, WE PRESS AHEAD."

The New Testament (Heb. 12:15-17) speaks of how Esau sold his birthright for a single meal and lived a life filled with regrets, unable to repent.

In a household of deception, we can't learn when God is teaching us because we have a stronghold determined to continue in a lie. We can't grow when God is stretching because, under pressure, we don't get stretched; we deceive to take the pressure off.

If you now realize that selfishness and deception was in your home of origin, what are you doing to ensure you are not passing those dysfunctions on to your children?

The discovery that we have been deceived and taught to deceive may unleash a toxic mixture of anger, shame, blaming, and revulsion toward our parents and grand-parents. We have already talked about the dangers of fault-finding in others when dysfunction is exposed in us. A wise response requires us to think differently.

If today's reading and thinking have been troublesome, remember that exposed strongholds have probably been in place for years, maybe decades. Don't expect instant demolishing. The wreckage may take years to clean up. Your initial temptation may be to think your situation is impossible. Take hope in Jesus' words, "With man this is impossible, but with God all things are possible" (Matt. 19:26).

MONEY-MATTERS-MORE STRONGHOLDS

Read Genesis 27:30-45. Note in particular the ways in which treasure or money plays a part in the way this story unfolds.

Genesis 27:30 begins like the instructions in a play. As Isaac, pretending to be Esau, leaves stage left, his brother, Esau, comes walking in stage right, back from his hunting. Esau has a huge platter on his shoulder, loaded down with the sizzling game he killed and prepared for his father.

After the identity confusion is sorted out, Isaac gives his eldest son the bad news. And Genesis 27:34 says, "As soon as Esau heard the words of his father, he cried out with an exceedingly great and bitter cry, 'Bless me, even me also, O my father!'"

It's hard to overstate how important it is for kids to get the blessing from their parents. There is an empty hole inside of us until those that brought us into this world will say, "I love you," "I'm for you," and "I'm thankful for you." By the way, that's one of the things that we should do for one another because a lot of people didn't get that in their home of origin. Our kindness to one another is part of God through us filling up what's lacking in each other's lives.

> **If you're living with the painful vacuum of never having gotten your parents' blessing, don't let that loss keep you from being a source of blessing in your children's and grandchildren's lives. How would your kids and grandkids answer if they were asked about receiving your blessing?**

In Genesis 27:37 Isaac told Esau, "Behold, I have made him lord over you, and all his brothers I have given to him for servants, and with grain and wine I have sustained him." Basically, "I gave Jacob all of my stuff. I don't have any stuff left for you."

Isaac's was a seriously "twisted, dysfunctional, strongholds everywhere" home, but I fully realize you maybe calling to mind something similarly twisted in your history. I don't bring it up callously or with indifference, only to gently say that nothing is going to change until it gets addressed. That stronghold is affecting the way that you think.

Let me just point out to you in this whole "get the blessing, the birthright, the livestock, the wine, the servants—get it all" setting indicates a non-monetary society. If this story was playing out today, it would be "get the 401k, the pension, the savings account, and the cabin in Wisconsin." There's the parallel. It's money. And the heading over this stronghold is money matters most.

Each of the family members had their own angle on the estate. Rebekah was thinking, *I just want the money to go to Jacob because he's my favorite.* For Jacob this was another step in his plan to lay hands on the inheritance, no matter how he had to treat his father. Isaac hit up Esau for a free meal and then wouldn't back off what he had done in being tricked into giving Jacob the blessing. We think, *Hey, Dad, how could he refuse Esau? You're the one that messed this up, blind guy. Fix this. You can pray for the other son. You can roll it back. You can say to Jacob, "You lied, Jacob, so you're out. Esau, you're back in the will."* Isaac could've done anything he wanted here, but he was stubborn and selfish. He held a lofty opinion of his importance that wouldn't let him say, "I was wrong." This was a money-matters-most family and it messed with all their other values.

Stubborn money strongholds are based on certain kinds of internal thinking. Below are five common ones. We can see these in Isaac's family, but we may well see them in our own families, too.

> **If one or more of these strikes close to home, own it and ask God to bring His power to bear on that stronghold.**

1. "I HAVE; THEREFORE, I AM."

In some families, the parents purchase, polish, and parade what they have so that the kids grow up thinking that happiness is stuff. That stronghold is present in epidemic proportions in our culture. We have to ask God to help us be honest because it's so hard to be honest with ourselves. When you see it clearly in others, just remember you have your own strongholds. We're not going to be judging each other about each other's strongholds. We just want to work on these things and begin to think differently.

2. "I COUNT; THEREFORE, I'M SAFE."

A money first dysfunction isn't always seen in the person who's spending a lot. I knew a guy a few years ago who, every year, said, "This year my wife and I are living on ten percent less than last year." Really?! Well, that's awesome if you need to do that. I don't know if he did or if he didn't, but by the time he had reported seven or eight years in a row, I wanted to ask, "Can we talk to your wife to see how this is going?"

Does this sound familiar? "We don't spend anything. That sound you hear is our pinched pennies screaming. Look at this coat. I bought this coat in 1981. It's as good as the day I bought it." No, it isn't. That's a bit freaky. God forgive us. The "haves" can be smug and polished and purchase and parade; the "have nots", who have the least, can be very consumed with the money-matters-most strongholds.

3. "I COVET; THEREFORE, I RESENT."

Exodus 20:17 says, "You shall not covet," but we do. We see what people have, and we think we have to have it. If we can't have it, they shouldn't have it either!

4. "I'M CONTENT; THEREFORE, I'M SUPERIOR."

There's a kind of unhealthy contentment that assumes our well-being is entirely the product of our efforts and even takes for granted God's present and future bless-ings. This wealth-based contentment doesn't do well under adversity. The attitude that says, "We don't need anything because we've provided well for ourselves," and neglects God supplying all we have, is ripe for great disappointment and in danger of judgment.

5. "I COMPARE; THEREFORE, I BORROW."

Comparisons with others and the availability of easy credit are a toxic mix. We have to catch up. We spend money we don't have, borrowed from our future. There is nothing wrong with having a mortgage on a house if you can afford it, but consumer debt with no assets to back it up is just foolishness. Too many of us live with the stronghold of buying things we can't afford on credit cards that we can't afford and then struggling to pay for them.

Today you should cut up that credit card and not get another one until it's all paid off or, in your case, maybe never. If you know you can't or won't do that, face the real possibility of a towering stronghold called money in your life.

Read 1 Timothy 6:9-10 today, and ask God to preserve you from the love of money and its dangers.

DAY 5
SEEING CLEARLY AND THINKING DIFFERENTLY

If we think about temperaments using the picture of each type driving a certain vehicle, we'd say the choleric is driving a steamroller, tending to move at one speed and straight ahead. Meanwhile, the sanguine is driving a Volkswagen bus with a surfboard on top, flowers on the side, shag carpet and eleven people inside. He's almost out of gas, but the sanguine doesn't notice because of the loud music and other distractions. They almost sideswipe the phlegmatic who is driving an electric car that is getting unbelievable mileage, which he would be super happy to tell you about. That car is clean and polished—please don't touch it. The melancholy knows little about the mechanics or maintenance of his car, but he likes the color and the interior design. The sound system is amazing for listening to the music he loves. All of these temperaments, of course, have strengths and weaknesses.

The choleric gets things done. The sanguine is so much fun. The phlegmatic is measured and faithful, and the melancholy makes the world a beautiful place. Thank God for each of these temperaments, including your own version.

Now I want to circle back to these and show you how they each have a way of thinking. Here is a summary of the large circle graph we used during the teaching session. Refer to it as you continue.

Temperament	Stronghold	Argument	Lofty Opinion	Think Differently	Helpful Scriptures
Choleric	Anger	I won't	God isn't just	Humility	James 4:4-10
Sanguine	Foolishness	I want	God isn't sufficient	Wisdom	Psalm 63
Phlegmatic	Fear	I can't	God isn't sovereign	Trust	Psalm 18:1-6
Melancholy	Despair	I doubt	God isn't good	Hope	2 Cor. 1:7-10

Cholerics's minds can easily develop discordant thinking. They're the people frequently in conflict. They see conflict as a barrier to getting things done. If you're a choleric, you have a lot of conflict in your life, and you don't even know all of it. Cholerics don't have any problem about standing up to anybody about anything.

The sanguine is very different from the choleric—though they are both extroverts. Sanguines are characterized by impulsive thinking. Sanguine is my temperament. Sanguines can be fun, playful, and enjoyable, but they turn fast. So they are a little more intermittently explosive. They have a weaker self-control. Depending on their secondary temperament, sanguines can be prone to addictions.

The phlegmatic often has to contend with anxious thinking. While we all have to get victory over worry, the phlegmatic person has an ongoing battle with that mindset. They are particularly troubled by Post Traumatic Stress Disorder (PTSD) and bouts of generalized anxiety. Even panic attacks can become consuming for phlegmatics.

The melancholy wrestles with depressive thinking related to the name of their temperament. They have highs and lows and can even battle dysthymia, which can refer to intermittent depression or major depression.

As I continue, please focus on your own temperament. Remember that in the center of the circle diagram back in the lesson notes is the word *sin*. All problems in my life, all problems in my family, and all the problems on the face of this world and in this church are result of sin.

Use the chart above in today's reading to locate the strongholds causing sin in your life as they relate to your temperament.

I had a dear friend on staff make me a little t-shirt (it's quite a few years ago now), but it was super helpful. It said: When I get angry, I lose. It's not a win; it's a loss.

The choleric is willful. The stronghold is anger, and the argument is "I won't." The dark side of a choleric's ability to issue orders and lead is an inability to take orders and follow.

Now this is an important note for all the temperaments. The "lofty opinion" in each temperament is a theology, as in "every lofty opinion raised against the knowledge of God" (2 Cor. 10:5). What fortifies the stronghold is bad theology—a wrong belief about God. Cholerics justify the stronghold of anger with the internal argument "I won't," and their lofty opinion is "God is not just."

Cholerics think, *God is not just*. I can't rely on Him; I have to handle, settle, or take care of this. Choleric? You are wrong in that thinking. God loves you. You can wait on Him. You don't have to take charge. So the captured and Christ-centered thinking for the choleric is humility, and that doesn't mean acting humble. The truly humble person is not thinking about himself at all; he's thinking about other people.

The sanguine's stronghold can be thoughtless and even reckless actions. While the choleric's argument is "I won't," the sanguine's is "I want," as in, "This is what I want to do." A sanguine's bad theology (lofty opinion) is that God is not sufficient or that God is not enough. A sanguine suspects that God's will and God's ways are not going to be fun enough or fulfilling enough.

In the phlegmatic's mind the stronghold is fear. If that's not your thing, that's hard to relate to. You may never be afraid of anything ever, but phlegmatics have a default setting in anxiety. Just like you battle anger or you make foolish decisions, the phlegmatic battles fear. While the choleric is saying, "I won't," and the sanguine is insisting, "I want," the phlegmatic is arguing, "I can't." That's the internal self-talk for them.

The phlegmatic's bad theology, their lofty opinion, is God is not sovereign; He's not in control and is not taking all of this to a better place. Taking this kind of thinking captive under Christ produces trust. The phlegmatic needs to trust God. Until you do, you will not be thinking differently.

Finally, the melancholy wrestles with despair. The melancholy's argument is "I doubt." That's the thought process in their own minds—they almost instinctively respond with doubt. Nothing is ever settled. If despair is your stronghold, then "I doubt" is your argument, and your bad theology is God is not good. A melancholy knows they are thinking differently when they are filled with hope.

Note that the chart includes a Bible passage related to each of the temperaments. Read the one that fits your temperament. Then reread the description of the stronghold, argument, and lofty opinion that characterize your disposition. Continue to pray for yourself and the rest of the group.

WEEK 5
ENDING DOUBLE-MINDEDNESS

Congratulations! We've reached the halfway point in our study. Thank you for participating in Think Differently. *May God already be doing amazing work in your life as you seek to love Him with your mind.*

Some of the issues exposed in the last couple of weeks may have come with crushing weight for some group members. As you gather, be sensitive to the pain of hurts, regrets, and awareness of difficulty ahead that may be on others' minds. Use the following questions to introduce the discussion while encouraging everyone to participate.

Now that we've spent weeks thinking about personal disposition and family dysfunctions, how do you understand in a deeper way the statement: "Nothing is different until you think differently"?

We have taken a hard look at strongholds, arguments, and lofty opinions related to each of our dispositions. What have you taken away from those insights?

We now know a lot more about how our family of origin and our dispositions affect our thinking and influence everything we do. We are now facing the challenge of taking "every thought captive to obey Christ" (2 Cor. 10:5). In this session, we are looking at the matter of whether or not we still want to see the changes in our lives that God promises He can bring about.

What are some of the problems that develop when a person can't decide?

To prepare for this session's teaching on "Ending Double-mindedness," read together the following verses:

> *If any of you lacks wisdom, let him ask God, who gives generously to all without reproach, and it will be given him. But let him ask in faith, with no doubting, for the one who doubts is like a wave of the sea that is driven and tossed by the wind. For that person must not suppose that he will receive anything from the Lord; he is a double-minded man, unstable in all his ways.*
> **JAMES 1:5-8**

WATCH

COMPLETE THE VIEWER GUIDE BELOW AS YOU WATCH DVD SESSION 5.

Double-mindedness is wanting two things that can't _____.

There are _____ people.

Double-mindedness creates _____.

Double-mindedness affects _____.

You have to _____ to think differently.

Life is _____ percent what happens to you and _____ percent on how you choose to deal with/think about it.

Hope is the _____ expectation of something _____ tomorrow.

Three reasons we stop hoping:

1. It's a _____ to hope.
2. It's _____.
3. It _____ to hope.

You have to take _____ that _____ your desire.

DISCUSS THE DVD SEGMENT WITH YOUR GROUP, USING THE QUESTIONS BELOW.

Has anyone in the group visited the Holy Land? If so, what was a lasting impression? Does anyone have the Holy Land on their "bucket list"? Why?

Why did Jesus ask the obviously needy man, "Do you want to be healed?"

Why was it important for Jesus to have the man carry away his "bed"?

How have you found ways to honor the principle of Sabbath in your life? What makes it difficult?

Back to applying Jesus' question to the man. Why is it crucial for us to really want to think differently?

James defined hope as "the confident expectation of something better tomorrow." How or why does this help you clarify hope in your own life? On the hope meter (1 being low; 10 being high), what level would you give your hopefulness right now?

In this session's teaching, James reminded us that hope is a hassle, it's hard, and it hurts. Choose one of these. Talk about how you've discovered that's true.

Application: As his final application, James reminded us that we have to take action that reinforces our desire to think differently. What actions have you already taken these weeks to reinforce your desire? What will you do this week? Take a few minutes with the group to pray with each other. Ask for God's help in desiring to think differently and in taking specific actions to reinforce that desire.

This week's Scripture memory:

> *If any of you lacks wisdom, let him ask God, who gives generously to all without reproach, and it will be given him. But let him ask in faith, with no doubting, for the one who doubts is like a wave of the sea that is driven and tossed by the wind. For that person must not suppose that he will receive anything from the Lord; he is a double-minded man, unstable in all his ways.* **JAMES 1:5-8**

Assignment: Complete the daily lessons for this next week as a thoughtful review of this session's teaching. Make a note of further questions or thoughts related to this week's lessons that you can share with other group members. Pray for each of your group by name, asking God to help them think differently this week.

We have been piling on the *Think Differently* issues for several weeks. We have been working to understand better not only how God made us but also the condition we are in because of sin's influence on our lives. We have been talking about thinking differently and we have been memorizing these verses related to the entire series:

> *For though we walk in the flesh, we are not waging war according to the flesh. For the weapons of our warfare are not of the flesh but have divine power to destroy strongholds. We destroy arguments and every lofty opinion raised against the knowledge of God, and take every thought captive to obey Christ, being ready to punish every disobedience, when your obedience is complete.*
> **2 CORINTHIANS 10:3-6**

I want to acknowledge that it's both healthy and hard to handle the load of these last few weeks. Hopefully you've discovered ways to share your struggles and bear the struggles of others as you have meet each session. I pray that the importance of thinking differently has been more and more on your mind. I got a text this week from someone who said, "I think about this several times a day: nothing is different until I think differently."

Nothing is different about a pattern of behavior that you want to break—something that has been hard for you—that you want to get victory over until you think differently.

I had planned to go back to the life of Jacob in this session and add to the two previous big lessons on strongholds (disposition and family of origin) this further one: strongholds of personal behavior, but I've had a sense that we are piling on so relentlessly about things that need to change that we would be wise to just stop right here and spend a week actually working on changing our thinking. Then we'll come back to the life of Jacob and the lessons from his life next week.

DAY 1
CONFRONTING DOUBLE-MINDEDNESS

James 1:5 tells us what to do when we realize we need wisdom (which should pretty much be most of the time): "If any of you lacks wisdom, let him ask God, who gives generously to all without reproach, and it will be given him." That's the need, the required action, the gracious source, and the promise. If the recurring thought you have been having more and more the last few weeks is *I need to think differently*, you have wandered into the awareness that James calls lacking wisdom. You may not yet be clear on what thinking differently will involve, but you realize that the way you have been thinking is no different from what the world thinks and what lost people think. You want to be done with that because you know that your thinking isn't taking you where you want to go.

You may already be familiar with James 1:2-4, but those verses are worth reading as you follow this discussion. We are most aware of our lack of wisdom when we come up against the hard things of life. And when God tells us to count trials joy and to think of hardship as opportunities to develop great qualities, we know immediately that God wants us to think differently.

A condition and explanation is added in verses 6-7: "But let him ask in faith, with no doubting, for the one who doubts is like a wave of the sea that is driven and tossed by the wind. For that person must not suppose that he will receive anything from the Lord." James completed the thought by naming the condition that prevents our requests for wisdom and for everything else to go nowhere: "He is a double-minded man, unstable in all his ways" (v. 8). The term *double-minded* is used only here and again by James in 4:8, Draw near to God, and he will draw near to you. Cleanse your hands, you sinners, and purify your hearts, you double-minded." James knew we have a problem with double-mindedness.

Double-mindedness, or literally having a double soul, means wanting two things that can't coexist. It's holding a pair of intentions or desires that contradict and can't both be true. For example, these two objectives desired don't go together, so they are classic statements of double-mindedness:

- □ **"I want a good marriage, but I want to keep on being selfish."**
- □ **"I want my private addiction, and I want a growing relationship with God."**
- □ **"I want my impulsive purchases at the mall, and I want financial stability and security."**
- □ **"I want my anger whenever I feel it and lasting, meaningful relationships."**
- □ **"I want my fears and anxieties, but I also want emotional stability and peaceful days."**

Those are all expressions of double-mindedness. They are probably not all echoes of your thinking, but several may be right on target in your life.

> **Pause for a moment as you read back through those five statements above. Check the ones that might be quotes from you. What other contradictory desires do you find yourself sometimes wanting? Ask God for the courage to confront double mindedness.**

Double-mindedness is a refusal to face a choice. We actually can't have our cake and eat it too. Our thinking has to change: "If I really want this, I'm not going to have that. I have to get off of the fence and stop with the in between. No more half measures. I have to settle this: What do I really want?" No more double-mindedness.

> **In what ways does your indecisiveness and unpredictability cause trouble for the people around you?**

Double-mindedness affects everything. It may show up clearly in one area, but it does its destructive work in other areas too. The guy who is double-minded about his marriage? It's affecting his career. The person who is double-minded about his finances? That's affecting his parenting. We can vehemently claim, "I might make a bad financial decision, but I would never do anything to hurt my family!" Yet the truth is we are actually doing harm to them. The highly compartmentalized and individualized life is just another way to describe a double-minded, multiple-minded, and confused-minded view of living. The rotten apple does spoil the bushel; the weak link does make the chain fail. What's James answer? It starts with, "If any of you lacks wisdom, let him ask God" (Jas. 1:5).

The apostle Paul, in Philippians 2:1-5, said, "Have this mind among yourselves which is yours in Christ Jesus" (v. 5). Follow the way he developed this single-minded emphasis as a shared way of thinking among the followers of Jesus:

> *So if there is any encouragement in Christ, any comfort from love, any participation in the Spirit, any affection and sympathy, complete my joy by being of the same mind, having the same love, being in full accord and of one mind. Do nothing from selfish ambition or conceit, but in humility count others more significant than yourselves. Let each of you look not only to his own interests, but also to the interests of others. Have this mind among yourselves, which is yours in Christ Jesus.*
> **PHILIPPIANS 2:1-5**

What are some of the ways we treat one another differently when we have the same mind according to Paul?

In the first verse Paul mentions five experiences that ought to motivate us toward the same mind of thinking differently. After each one, jot how that particular one would help motivate you:

Encouragement in Christ:

Comfort from love:

Participation in the Spirit:

Affection:

Sympathy:

I'm challenging you to locate an area of double-mindedness in your life and make a decision about it before you close this workbook today. Pray now, "God, show me what that is, and help me eliminate it."

DAY 2
DO I WANT THIS?

For this change-of-pace lesson we're going to walk with Jesus into an encounter with someone who had been in desperate need for a long time—thirty-eight years. He was stuck. His case was an obvious example of someone Jesus could help. We are about to meet a man who needs to think differently.

Open your Bible to follow along as we study John 5:1-15. You may notice that your copy of the Scriptures may or may not have verse four included in the main text. If it isn't, you will find it in the footnotes. This is a rare case in which the most reliable copies of the New Testament manuscripts don't include this particular verse, even though the clarifying detail mentioned in the verse is included later in the account. The first six verses set up the encounter:

> *After this there was a feast of the Jews, and Jesus went up to Jerusalem. Now there is in Jerusalem by the Sheep Gate a pool, in Aramaic called Bethesda, which has five roofed colonnades. In these lay a multitude of invalids—blind, lame, and paralyzed. One man was there who had been an invalid for thirty-eight years. When Jesus saw him lying there and knew that he had already been there a long time, he said to him, "Do you want to be healed?"*
> **JOHN 5:1-6**

Do we agree that Jesus put a fairly unusual question to a person who has been waiting thirty-eight years to be healed? Why would Jesus ask him that?

Or, because it's Jesus asking the question, can we assume there is something deeper going on in this situation?

Based on your exposure to Jesus Christ, why would you expect Him to ask this question?

While we're pondering the situation, the man responds, but he doesn't answer Jesus' question: "The sick man answered him, 'Sir, I have no one to put me into the pool when the water is stirred up, and while I am going another steps down before me.'" (v. 7). Isn't that the way it always is with a person when the floodgates open and a torrent of feelings pour out? This guy has been thinking this for thirty-eight years. How often did someone come up to him and ask, "Do you want to be healed?" It just never happened. But he had developed this mindset that substitutes the answer to the question Jesus asked with the answer to the question, "Why haven't you been healed?" The mixture of frustration and despair just came gushing out of him, "Well, because every time the water gets stirred and I try to get in someone else beats me. I never move up in line because there is no line! It's every invalid for himself; I don't have anyone to help me get in."

How does this explanation compare to the way you talk about disappointments in your life?

For decades this guy had been watching other people who haven't been at the pool as long as he has or don't even have a big of a need as he does getting in and getting healed, and he's not. How does that feel? It was obvious to Jesus: "Jesus said to him, 'Get up, take up your bed, and walk'" (v. 8).

But,if you had been laying there for thirty-eight years and Jesus came and said to you, "Get up and walk," you would. That makes total sense. The part that I don't get is Jesus mentioning the bed.

There are now two things that you should be reflecting on: 1) Why did Jesus ask him, "Do you want to be healed?" and 2) Why did Jesus tell him to bring his bed with him? We'll come back to them later this week.

Beginning in John 5:9 the great thing happens and is immediately ignored as an amazing demonstration of God's power:

And at once the man was healed, and he took up his bed and walked. Now that day was the Sabbath. So the Jews said to the man who had been healed, "It is the Sabbath, and it is not lawful for you to take up your bed." But he answered them, "The man who healed me, that man said to me, 'Take up your bed, and walk.'" They asked him, "Who is the man who said to you, 'Take up your bed and walk'?" Now the man who had been healed did not know who it was, for Jesus had withdrawn, as there was a crowd in the place.

JOHN 5:9-13

The guys confronting the healed man were always in conflict with Jesus over the Sabbath. In their minds and according to their little rule list, healing and carrying one's bed on Sabbath were forbidden actions. Good news; wrong day. They wanted to be in charge even if it meant telling God what He could and couldn't do on the Sabbath.

The healed man didn't even know who Jesus was. So, did this guy get saved? No, he did not get saved; he just got healed. But Jesus tracked him down and gave him an opportunity far more valuable than his healing: "Afterward Jesus found him in the temple and said to him, 'See, you are well! Sin no more, that nothing worse may happen to you'" (v. 14). Jesus wasn't saying that his sin made him sick and that if he sinned again he was going to get sicker. Jesus was saying, "You have a pattern of sin in your life that has never been interrupted. So even though you're healed after thirty-eight years, if you don't get healed at a deeper level, you're going to a place in eternity that's going to make thirty-eight years of waiting look like a vacation." There is something deeper that has to happen.

For some in this study, the decision that you need to make, once and for all, is to get off the fence and give your life to Christ and start following Him. How have you resolved the matter of your own need for a Savior from sin?

If you've trusted in Christ as your Savior, how has that relationship allowed you to think differently? After all, hope is a byproduct of thinking differently.

DAY 3
WHAT IS HOPE?

The objective of this entire study will be missed if you never get the point that you have to really want to think differently. You have to recognize that the world around you is thinking one way, but now you are ready to apply your mind in a different direction, toward God and His Word.

I can't do that for you. I hope that you can sense from me throughout these lessons that I care for you. If I could make you want to think differently, I'd do it. I'm trying to motivate you. I'm laboring to give you every compelling reason available to change your mind about all God has in store for you. But at the end of the day, you have to choose. You're the one who's deciding how to think about everything that happens in your life.

At this point in the study would you say you have made some definite changes in your thinking or are you still waiting to be convinced that a change is necessary?

Someone once said that life is 10 percent what happens to you, 90 percent on how you choose to deal with it. Or to put it another way, living is 90 percent on how you choose to think about it. You have to care about your assumptions and responses. You have to still be hoping for something better in your life. One of the driving forces to get you and keep you thinking differently is hope.

Think of some examples from your own life, examples that illustrate differences between what happened and how you responded to it.

When a bad storm comes and floods the entire neighborhood, are you one of those who hunkers down waiting to be rescued or one of those getting out your chainsaw and launches your boat to rescue your neighbors? How are those two mindsets different?

I hope you realize that when you've lost hope, you've lost everything. There is nothing after "no hope." Here's a definition of the word *hope*: the confident expectation of something better tomorrow. Hope isn't necessarily about instant results; it's more open-ended than that. But hope creates a reason for decisions and choices today that depends on the confidence that they will be proven right and worthwhile tomorrow.

Farmers are full of hope. They look at their empty, muddy fields in the spring and they picture an abundant harvest in the fall. They till the soil and plant the seeds in hope. Even though nothing happens for several weeks, they remain confident. Their hope is rewarded by the blush of green that covers the field as the tender plants break through the ground.

Followers of Jesus practice the greatest hope of all. Authentic Christians are those who know that, no matter how many peaks and valleys we go through in our lives, this whole thing is heading fast toward a massive, forever celebration. We're fired up about heaven, and we're looking forward to being with Christ. The world sees only a hopeless end; we see an endless hope. That's Christianity. Not just a distant eternity, but actually seeing God involved now meeting needs, answering prayers, carrying burdens, relieving me of sin, changing my life, and increasing my joy on the journey to that endless hope. People ought to notice this quality in our lives. In fact, the apostle Peter told us our hope should open doors to share the gospel with people. He said, "But in your hearts honor Christ the Lord as holy, always being prepared to make a defense to anyone who asks you for a reason for the hope that is in you; yet do it with gentleness and respect" (1 Peter 3:15).

What would the people who know you best say about the quality of your hope?

When was the last time someone asked you, "How come you're so hopeful all the time?"

If someone did ask you about your hope, what would you say? As Peter would ask, "How are you prepared with a reason?"

Do Christians lose hope? Yes, they do. The story we studied yesterday was in part an account of a man losing hope. I kind of joked when I asked, "Was that a good question to ask, 'Do you want to be healed?'" That was actually a brilliant question for Jesus to ask. What Jesus was saying to the man was, "Do you still want this?"

How long was the guy by that pool? Where were you 38 years ago? Four decades ago I was in eighth grade. You may not have even been alive 38 years ago. Furthermore, in New Testament times, the life expectancy was only 40 years. I don't know how old this kid was when he was dropped off at there, but someone got him to the pool and left him to live alone because he told Jesus he had "no one" to help him.

But he did have that stirred up water. So how many times did the water get stirred in the first year and he didn't get in it? How many times did he see other people see improvements in their health or healing and he was just watching other people have what he wanted? Maybe after the first year, he thought, *I'm going to find a way. I'm going to get somebody to help me move this body into that water.* He was still hopeful.

But what was he thinking in year 10? *I've been here longer than ANYBODY now. It has to be MY turn.*

What was he thinking in year 20? Had he gotten a little cynical or angry? He was still lying there 10 years after that, celebrating his 30th anniversary at the pool; now what did he think about all of this? Did he still say he's going to get healed? Did he still think, *My time's coming. It's not my time yet.* What was he thinking in year 35? Someone was keeping count of the years.

Here's the point: The biggest thing that you may be battling during this study is that you have been thinking the way that you have been thinking for a long time.

In the passage of time what gets lost is hope. When you stop hoping for something different, it is definitely not coming. When you stop hoping, you stop caring, and perhaps you will never think differently. Nothing will change.

THREE CHALLENGES TO HOPE

I hope you can remember from the teaching session a few days ago that there are three reasons why we stop hoping. But I'd like to encourage you to think through them again, pausing to consider how each of these obstacles or challenges may be draining or sucking the hope out of your life.

Yesterday we defined hope as the confident expectation of something better tomorrow. Hope looks forward, with faith, which is what confidence means, but we also acknowledged that even Christians can have their hope diminished to the point of apparent extinction. And when we backtrack the falling trajectory of our hope, we usually find some or all of the following factors played a part in wearing down of hope and preventing us from seeking those things that energize it.

THE HASSLE OF HOPE

First, we often stop hoping because it is a hassle to hope. Even the best spiritual routine that you and I might develop can become a stifling or uncomfortable weight. Watch how it happens:

You get up in the morning, thanking God for the new day. You open God's Word and continue a pattern of reading that allows God to speak to you. You spend time in prayer and get focused for the day. Then you go out to face the world super positive.

You walk into your school, into your work, or into whatever you do, and you're fired up and trusting God because you have prepared yourself for the hours ahead.

Then someone shows up and says, "What's wrong with you? I don't know why you're so positive. Have you got your head stuck in sand? Look at this world. It's going to hell in a handbasket!"

You had a hopeful outlook, and they just sucked the hope right out of you. They stepped into your life with a portable hope vacuum and extracted every particle of hope from you. Just when you get yourself in a place of faith, and just when you get yourself in a place of trusting God, somebody comes along and just goes right after it.

What is your strategy for resisting having your hope vacuumed away?

HOPE IS HARD

As I just mentioned, hoping involves an effort. It requires a deliberate choice in the face of loud and persistent voices demanding hopelessness. Hope is not the default position. You have to work on hope. It's hard. It is actually work, and it starts over every morning.

Nobody works at negativity. No one says, "Hey! Just leave me alone! When I come back in an hour I'll be so negative you're not going to believe it. I need a little time to whip up my critical attitude."

No real effort is involved in generating negativity. It just shows up, right? You don't ever work at that, but you work at hope. You have to actually discipline your mind. Because it's so easy to think hopelessly, you have to train your mind to think differently.

And if we're not careful, for example, in regard to people, we lose hope in people and get critical. We find ourselves thinking, *I just don't believe that she's changing. I just don't believe that he's ever going to be different.* That's not how God feels about us, but we form that conclusion about others because we lose hope in them. And that is so wrong.

Criticism flows when we lose hope in people; complaining erupts when we lose hope in circumstances. Both reveal we have anchored our hope too much in what can only provide partial encouragement. So we end up thinking, *Why is this like this? When is this situation going to be different? I don't like these circumstances anymore. I can't do this anymore.* Those rapid-fire, demanding questions reveal a critical and complaining attitude development because we've lost hope.

I understand—hope is hard. The Bible says, "Hope deferred makes the heart sick" (Prov. 13:12).

You may be saying, "I have tried for a long time. I believed for a long time. The stuff on my hope list doesn't seem to be happening."

I know—but what I'm trying to show you is that when you give up hope, you give up so much. You won't be better off over on this hard self-protected "nothing is ever going to change" attitude. That is not a better place to be. Hope is protecting God's best future for you.

What are some of the situations or places in your life where hope is hard to maintain?

How do you think things would change if you began to think differently about those situations?

HOPE HURTS

Hoping may be a hassle and it may be hard, but the biggest reason why we stop hoping is because it hurts to hope. When we hope, we make ourselves vulnerable to being disappointed.

But that awesome place of vulnerability is where God has done the most in your life. You need to go back to that awesome place of hope, not because of a confidence ultimately based on people (including yourself) or circumstances but a hope anchored to a great God who loves you and has the best plans for you.

How are you responding to the point above that in the long run it hurts a lot more not to hope and to hope?

Before you begin tomorrow's homework, spend some time thinking about the way your hope has been affected by double-mindedness in your life. Ask God to show you places where you have yielded to the pressures of hassles, hardship, and pain, resulting in a weak or lost hope.

DAY 5
TAKING ACTION

Back in week 1 of this series, we noted that the final obstacle to thinking differently was the necessity of personal engagement. Here we are again. Not only do we need to want to think differently, we have to take actions that reinforce that desire. This is particularly true if our temperament trends toward passivity or if our family of origin dysfunctions have trained us to respond passively to the world around us. It's a problem if we're assuming things will just happen rather than making necessary choices that will lead to change.

If you want to think differently, you have to take action that reinforces your desire. You can say that you want to think differently forever, but until you actually do some things that demonstrate your full intention to change, it's not going to happen. The process is like dreaming of sailing around the world or the desire to get married. At some point dreaming doesn't matter if you never learn to sail, get a boat, and cast off from the dock. The desire for marriage loses its purpose if you never ask the girl and set the date.

> **What are some choices you need to make that you've left sitting in the desire position for too long? Determine for each what would be a first real step you could take to act on that desire.**

Ending double-mindedness has to move beyond private wishing to some kind of public actions that announce: "Do you see me? I've been in a cycle. I've been kind of stuck. But I'm making a big choice here so that I can get to an even better place."

Some of the hardest and most courageous decisions are the decisions to take action to get to a place where you can think differently. That's why Jesus told this guy at the pool, "Get up, take up your bed, and walk" (John 5:8). That was the abbreviated way of Jesus saying, "Because you're not coming back here do something physical to reinforce your decision. You're taking that bed to the landfill. The kind of thinking and living that you had until this morning is over. You laid by that pool for thirty-eight years. You are done with that. You're not coming back here, and you're not leaving any sign that you were here. That's behind you now. You're going on into something new, something better."

Pause at this point before reading the rest of today's homework. We're only halfway through our lessons about thinking differently, but it's time for a reality check about choices you're making along the way.

You can keep your distance during these sessions and see them as merely the gathering of information and spiritual insights that ultimately apply to other people but not to you. Or, you can humble yourself by admitting that you've got some temperament issues that will have to be addressed and some family dysfunctions that you honestly don't want to pass on to the next generation.

The fact that this feels like a serious, rest-of-your-life-moment may cause some anxiety, but don't let that deter you from answering the "What step am I ready to take at this moment?" question. This is what I frequently call "the crisis" before "the process" that must follow. Change rarely happens if we try to process ourselves into thinking differently; there has to be a crisis—a clear, intense, deliberate moment of decision that is made in the sight of God and others. It clears the ground of our lives for the new structure the process will build as God guides us.

Are you ready for the crisis? If you are, let's start with first things first. Have you made the decision to follow Jesus Christ?

If you know you've never made that deliberate choice, do you believe that Jesus Christ is God's Son? Do you believe that He died to pay for the penalty for your sin? If you do believe those two facts, you must take some action beyond mental agreement. If you know you are not reconciled to God through faith in His Son Jesus, that can change right now. Maybe you've been hanging around the edge of Christianity or you've been on-and-off and in-and-out but not really become a devoted follower of Jesus. The best thing that you could do is to end the double-mindedness, pick up your phone, and call the leader of your small group, your pastor, or another member of the group you know is a believer and tell them this:

I am taking a big step I know I need to take in order to think differently. I'm yielding my life to Jesus Christ today. I am recognizing Him as my Savior and Lord. I'm ready to consider my life completely in His hands and my relationship right with Him. I'm coming today to settle, once and for all, that I am placing my faith and trust in Jesus. I am determined to follow Him because He died for me and provided me with forgiveness for my sins. I accept that forgiveness and I accept Him.

Jesus said, "So everyone who acknowledges me before men, I also will acknowledge before my Father who is in heaven" (Matt. 10:32). By telling others about your decision you will be confirming it in your own heart and mind. You will be carrying out the crisis Paul described in Romans 10:9-10, "If you confess with your mouth that Jesus is Lord and believe in your heart that God raised him from the dead, you will be saved. For with the heart one believes and is justified, and with the mouth one confesses and is saved."

One of the biblical ways of confessing is being baptized. Very few things say "I'm thinking differently about everything" than going under the waters of baptism in a public setting. To be clear, baptism is not how you get saved; it's what saved people do. It's a simple, clear step of obedience that puts into action our decision to place our faith in Jesus Christ.

If you've never been baptized, even if you've been a believer in Jesus for many years, now is a good time to get that taken care of. Contact your pastor to participate in whatever preparation classes are part of the process, but don't put off the opportunity to declare before the world that your hope and your life are in Christ.

If you have been a baptized believer for a short or long time, what you have been experiencing during these *Think Differently* sessions may be a mini-crisis of getting things right in certain areas of life or a reminder by God's Spirit that the process of sanctification is not finished in your life. Philippians 1:6 says, "And I am sure of this, that he who began a good work in you will bring it to completion at the day of Jesus Christ."

Ask God to continue to open your eyes to ways you can think differently and make you humble enough to depend on Him for the changes that need to happen in order for you to see your mind changed.

WEEK 6

STRONGHOLDS OF MY OWN MAKING

Welcome to week 6 of Think Differently, *in which we are continuing to discover how to really change our minds.*

Last week was a time of regrouping and personalizing of the lessons, take a few minutes for group members to share any thoughts or decisions related to the homework from the last few days. Use the following questions to expand the discussion while encouraging everyone to participate.

As we dive into the second half of this series, tell the rest of the group how they can be praying for you in the weeks to come.

Describe one way you are thinking differently about God than you did when this study began.

In what way did your disposition or your family of origin dysfunctions play a significant part in an event this past week? (Either keeping you out of trouble or dropping you in hot water.)

Let's not get tired of reminding ourselves that nothing is really going to be different until we think differently. We are learning week by week that our thinking influences everything we do. This week we're back into the life of Jacob to see the way God's Word shows us, through that flawed man, the lessons He has for us, who are equally flawed.

To prepare for this session and continue to memorize the foundational passage for the series, read together the following verses:

> *For though we walk in the flesh, we are not waging war according to the flesh. For the weapons of our warfare are not of the flesh but have divine power to destroy strongholds. We destroy arguments and every lofty opinion raised against the knowledge of God, and take every thought captive to obey Christ, being ready to punish every disobedience, when your obedience is complete.*
> **2 CORINTHIANS 10:3-6**

WATCH

COMPLETE THE VIEWER GUIDE BELOW AS YOU WATCH DVD SESSION 6.

The most powerful driving force behind the strongholds that trip us up and take us down is our own _____.

Strongholds show up when we _____ what we have _____.

One of the surest signs of a _____ is seeing _____ in the sins of others.

The Stronghold Rule: Others will _____ to you as you have _____ to others.

Strongholds blow up through our own _____.

Do any of the common 12 strongholds sound familiar? Check any that apply.

☐ **Anger**   ☐ **False Guilt**   ☐ **Fear**
☐ **Covetous**   ☐ **Rebellion**   ☐ **Unbelief**
☐ **Control**   ☐ **Pride**   ☐ **Skepticism**
☐ **Individualism**   ☐ **Idolatry**   ☐ **Escapism**

Jacob didn't have to keep _____ with God.

Jacob didn't have to keep _____ his family.

Jacob didn't have to keep _____.

Jacob didn't have to keep avoiding _____.

Strongholds grow up in the _____ of loved ones.

If nothing else scares us into _____ the strongholds in our lives, seeing them in our _____ _____ should.

DISCUSS THE DVD SEGMENT WITH YOUR GROUP, USING THE QUESTIONS BELOW.

Take a quick look at your notes from James' review of the first sessions of *Think Differently*. Which point caused you think something like "I need to remember this"? Why?

What would it be like to have someone like Jacob for a neighbor?

As you consider the principle that others will do to you what you have done to others, what instances in your life does that describe?

When have you seen God allow unexpected or unusual things to happen that advanced His purpose in your life or someone else's?

James pointed out from the text four repeated behaviors that Jacob didn't have to keep doing: bargaining with God, neglecting family, deceiving others, and avoiding conflict. Which one(s) of these need special attention in your life? Why?

When have you noticed of your children or others emulating/imitating either your good or bad behavior?

Do you agree or disagree with James' statement: "The most powerful driving force behind the strongholds that trip us up and take us down is our own behavior?" Why or why not?

Application: Take a few minutes to pray with each other asking for God's help in making the changes of behavior that will have to come with thinking differently.

This week's Scripture memory:

> *Do not be deceived: God is not mocked, for whatever one sows, that will he also reap.* **GALATIANS 6:7**

Assignment: Complete the daily lessons for this next week in order to benefit from the insights in the lesson. Make a note of further questions or thoughts related to this week's teaching that you can share with other group members. Again, make it a daily habit to pray for each person of your group by name, asking God to help them think differently this week.

STRONGHOLDS OF MY OWN MAKING

At this point in the series, we've all got strongholds on our minds. We know we have them, we suspect we can't recognize many of them, and we're getting serious about having God demolish them—because we can't.

We now know that strongholds, when we find them, can be traced back to one of three sources:

- **Disposition strongholds** are bent places in our disposition. God gives us a certain temperament, and the effects of sin in the world—and in us—bends and distorts our disposition. We looked at four broad dispositions and 16 possible combinations, since each of us has a major one and a secondary one. Our dispositions can't be changed, but the strongholds of resistance to God's Word and God's ways can be demolished.

- **Family dysfunction strongholds** begin through family dysfunction. Our interactions with our parents and siblings establish some unique fortresses and reinforce strongholds in our dispositions. Families are a complex puzzle of temperaments, all affecting one another for good or bad.

- Our **behavior strongholds** build through our own behaviors. We vote with our bent disposition and willfully participate in family dysfunctions. That's reality. Regardless of my bent, and regardless of how I began and where I was born, at the end of the day what all of this comes down to is: I am building or destroying; I am rising up against the knowledge of God or I am tearing down strongholds in my life—and it all comes down to my own thinking.

Now wouldn't it be easy if we could blame our strongholds on God? "Hey, God, You gave me this disposition. How can you hold me responsible when You made me this way?" And wouldn't it be easy if we could blame our strongholds on our parents? "Man! My parents and the home I grew up in—that was a stronghold factory!" But thinking about who we can blame for the strongholds in our lives is not thinking differently; finding fault with others comes automatically.

DAY 1
SOWING AND REAPING

Take a few minutes to read Genesis 29:1-30. As you read, track the way God blesses His chosen patriarch and notice how the strongholds also appear in the story. Jacob has left home and traveled to Haran, the homeland of his mother's family. He marries the two daughters of Laban and begins a family.

Jacob's name means deceiver. He was a liar and a cheater. It's what he had always done to get what he wanted. It was a major stronghold in his life. Now God confront ed that stronghold by causing Jacob to experience what others felt when he did that to them.

The Golden Rule says: "As you wish that others would do to you, do so to them: (Luke 6:31). This was Jesus' baseline instruction for human interaction. The rule is in contrast to a related principle we could call the Stronghold Rule: Others will do to you as you have done to others. You can bank on that. The world calls it, "What goes around comes around." The Bible describes the process in Galatians 6:7: "For whatever one sows, that will he also reap."

However you want to say it, generations and civilizations have observed the unalterable principle that God Himself installed in human behavior. And it is this: Strongholds show up in our lives and we begin to reap what we have sown.

If you're a parent, what tendencies or expressions can you see in your children that they must have picked up from you?

What decisions did your parents make that you can see are positive or negative examples of reaping what they sowed?

In his mother's brother, Laban, Jacob met his deceptive equal. Once he realized the Jacob was head over heels for Rachel, Laban manipulated Jacob into committing to work for seven years in exchange for Rachel's hand in marriage. A hint of Jacob's smitten state can be seen in the description of those waiting years, "So Jacob served seven years for Rachel, and they seemed to him but a few days because of the love he had for her" (Gen. 29:20). But when the time was up and the wedding feast was in full swing, Laban substituted Leah for Rachel, and Jacob consummated his marriage to the wrong woman. In the morning, Jacob was shocked and angry with Laban, who calmly told him, basically, "Didn't you read the memo about our traditions? The oldest is always married before the younger. But here's what I'll do. Wait a week and I'll give you Rachel also, as long as you work for me another seven years" (see Gen. 29:21-27). With a sleight of hand, Laban pulled two fast ones on Jacob. He was either very clever, or there were other factors at play in this clash of strongholds.

Think for a moment about the moment of realization for the future patriarch. "And Jacob said to Laban, 'What is this you have done to me? Did I not serve with you for Rachel? Why then have you deceived me?'" (Gen. 29:25). Ding! Ding! Ding! The weight of reality's boulder has landed on Jacob's head. And right in that second—"Why then have you deceived me?"—he realized "It has happened! I am reaping what I have sown. I am feeling what I have made others feel."

The liar has been lied to. The cheater has been cheated. The deceiver has been deceived. A stronghold had been revealed. What's interesting is, in the remainder of this exchange with Laban, Jacob didn't say another word. He had been beaten at his own game. He nods agreement to Laban's proposal. I believe Jacob was crushed with the realization of what it's like on the receiving end of deception. Jacob was living what the prophet Hosea warned, "They sow the wind, and they shall reap the whirlwind" (Hos. 8:7). His previous poor choices had come back upon Jacob.

Let your criticism of your parents show you yourself. Let your fears for your children take you deeper into destroying the strongholds of fear in your own life.

Where are you in the process of reaping what you have sown?

How will you break the chains, the strongholds, for the next generation?

Regrets can lead to repentance, but they are not the same thing as repentance. Regrets sadly contemplate a terrible harvest of evil sown. Regrets realize that even good things sown have been choked out and destroyed like healthy plants being overcome by weeds or a crop being consumed by insects. Regrets, even when shared with others, are helpless acknowledgments that we could have done better but it's too late.

But repentance begins with the moment of regret and moves toward God. Repentance realizes we can't change the past but that God can. God is, first of all, the God who loves and forgives. Repentance is helpless reliance on God's mercy and His capacity, not to change the past but to alter the results of what we have done in the past.

> **As you are realizing the strongholds of your own making, don't let regrets be your stopping point. Ask God to show you where repentance is necessary.**

Restoration is under God's control and His timing. Once repentance has been expressed, trust God and let Him guide your steps forward.

Jacob apparently lived silently with his regrets. We don't see evidence of repentance in his actions. In fact, we will see as the week progresses that, in many ways, Jacob simply continued under the direction of his strongholds even when part of him was attempting to obey God.

God's salvation plan proceeded with Jacob in spite of the patriarch's many short-comings. It is healthy for us to remember that God accounts for all our screw-ups and never allows us to have the final word on how things work out in His will and His plans. Our choices and the resulting strongholds complicate a lot of things for us; they never complicate things for God.

> **Pause as you end today's assignment and thank God for His sovereignty in your life. Ask Him to remind you that He remains in control no matter what you are facing.**

WHEN STRONGHOLDS BLOW UP

Yesterday's events in the life of Jacob were an episode in "Truth Is Stranger than Fiction." Or maybe you saw it as a train wreck where everyone survived, but the trauma and the injuries were long-lasting. From the time Jacob met God in the place he called Bethel until the time following his marriage to Leah and Rachel, the Lord's presence or guidance is not acknowledged at all. Jacob is running his life, using his best thinking. As we have discovered in past lessons, we need to take note of where our best thinking has gotten us.

Jacob was reeling under the realization of reaping the harvest of his past decisions. I believe that God wanted Jacob to experience what Esau experienced after he ate the stew, after he lost his birthright. I believe that God wanted Jacob to experience what Isaac experienced when he realized that he had been deceived by his wife and his second son. And somehow God allowed this to happen. We don't have to put too much on alcohol or on the darkness in the bridal suite. We can put it on God because He is in control. Because God is in control, Jacob reaped what he sowed.

What are some recent difficult or improbable experiences God has allowed into your life to get your attention?

What have been the results?

During the DVD session I included twelve fairly common strongholds in people's lives that tend to create a harvest of bitter results. Here's that list again:

1. Anger. If your stronghold is anger, your thinking would be, *I need my anger to get things done. My anger gets me moving, and other people too! I rely on anger because it works!*

2. **Covetousness.** When your strongholds include covetousness, money and possessions mean security. Security presents itself as a sure way to happiness, so the need to accumulate money becomes your driving force, colored with envy of what others have.

3. **Control.** Sometimes a stronghold shows up as a need to be in total control. This may be expressed as a fear of getting hurt, resistance to helplessness, or terror of exposure. The thought, *I have to be in control*, reveals this stronghold.

4. **Individualism.** This is your stronghold when you think that the only person you can truly count on is yourself. *I don't let others in. I don't ask for prayer. I take care of myself.*

5. **False guilt.** Do you think every bad thing that happens to you is punishment for your past and the choices you made? The gospel shouts that all of the punishment for our sin is upon Christ. But the stronghold of false guilt says, "Not so! Not you! God is still punishing you."

6. **Rebellion.** This stronghold says, "No one tells me what to do. I do what I want to do. I don't care what it costs. This is the most important thing: I get my way."

7. **Pride.** Perhaps you think you're better than everyone else. You don't owe anyone anything. You're first and the only name on the list. Those are the thoughts of a stronghold of pride: *Let's have more of me and less of anyone else.*

8. **Idolatry.** This stronghold is all about: *I have to have this. I need it. I deserve it. It's everything to me.* Is that a stronghold for you—something in the place of God?

9. **Fear.** This stronghold begins with reasonable caution but ends up near paranoia: *Something bad might be coming. I have to see it. I have to anticipate it. I have to stop it. I have to think about it all the time and be prepared for the worst.*

10. **Unbelief.** The stronghold of lack of faith can become entrenched: *Nothing is settled. Nothing is certain. Everything is random. All is hopeless. I don't believe. I can't believe.*

11. **Skepticism.** Deeply held suspicions can turn into an imposing stronghold by thinking, *Nobody cares. Everyone is trying to get something from me. No one is sincere. Everyone is a cheat. No one plays by the rules.* Skepticism is such a stronghold.

12. Escapism. Fake relief is offered as a real answer to build this stronghold. Fake relief urges us to smoke the joint, drain the bottle, join the party, take more vacations, dull the pain, blindly follow any path that offers a way out—and don't ever ask about the destination.

> **Read through the list again, asking God to help you see specific strongholds that may be controlling aspects of your life. Put a check next to those that seem likely candidates.**

> **Now, read the list again. Put a star next to any stronghold in someone's life that appears to be affecting your relationship with them and their relationships with others.**

Those are all massive strongholds. What an important subject we're studying! What an immense opportunity to see God's transforming power released in our lives, our small group, and our church! Nothing is different until we think differently.

Keep in mind that discovering your strongholds is the first step—just the first step—to destroying them.

> **Take a few minutes to work on memorizing this week's verse. Think about the ways our strongholds can put us in danger of mocking God. We have to think differently and soberly about our condition before the One who made us, knows us, and loves us.**

> *Do not be deceived: God is not mocked, for whatever one sows, that will he also reap.*
> **GALATIANS 6:7**

DAY 3
STAYING THE BAD COURSE

Begin your assignment for today by reading Genesis 28:10-22.

Over the next two days we are going to look at Jacob's life and four strongholds that God graciously revealed, but Jacob refused to leave behind. The first one is found in the passage you just read. God made Himself known to Jacob and made promises to the future patriarch. Jacob didn't have to keep bargaining with God, but he did.

We join Jacob on his journey to find a wife: "Jacob left Beersheba and went toward Haran. And he came to a certain place and stayed there that night, because the sun had set. Taking one of the stones of the place, he put it under his head and lay down in that place to sleep" (vv. 10-11). That is like the anti-pillow, but it's what Jacob did. Somehow, he slept. And then he had a dream during which he saw a ladder between earth and heaven, with angels ascending and descending. God stood at the top and spoke to Jacob (see vv. 12-13).

Nothing random was happening here. Jacob was shown something that no one else had seen. But Jacob doesn't get it, and we know this because of what he says in verse 20. God gave our slumbering traveler this amazing vision and told Jacob that He would multiply him—the reiteration of the Abrahamic Covenant. Abraham's grandson was the third generation to hear God's promise to build a nation, even though Jacob isn't married yet.

What's remarkable to me is that Jacob woke up frightened and in awe. He called that place the House of God—that's where the word *Bethel* comes from (Beth-El; House-God), which is why a lot of churches are called Bethel.

But notice Genesis 28:20, "Then Jacob made a vow, saying, 'If God will be with me ... ' " If? God just told him that He would be with him. He just appeared to Jacob in a dream and told him that He would be with him. Jacob's response was, "If God will be with me and will keep me in this way that I go, and will give me bread to eat ... " His first thought was to negotiate now for bread and clothes when God just promised to give him everything?

Why do you think people try to strike bargains with God rather than accept His grace?

You see, Jacob's response is a stronghold of figuring the angles and trying to come out ahead. He can't stop negotiating. Jacob can't stop representing himself. Here he was basically telling God, "Well, You said You would do everything for me, but I want to stipulate these two little things (a fraction of what God had just promised) and make sure Your promise includes them. If You'll just make sure I have clothes and food, then You can be my God. O, and bring me back here safely so I can return home in peace. I'll name this place Your home and I will tithe what you've given me."

It was just awful—Jacob's thinking was a stronghold. He didn't have to keep bargaining with God. Jacob didn't have to do that. But for some reason, Jacob continued to negotiate.

Jacob didn't have it settled. Jacob knows about God. The strongholds were still standing, and they were showing up in his decisions.

When do you find yourself tempted to negotiate with God? Read Genesis 29:31–30:24.

A second example of Jacob's strongholds that could have been demolished by thinking differently had to do with his home life. Jacob kept neglecting his family.

Keep in mind that Abraham was told that his descendants were going to be like the sands by the seashore. Have you ever tried to count a handful of sand, let alone a whole beach? But in generation two, he has exactly one descendant named Isaac. In generation three, because Esau was out, it was just going to be Jacob. But Jacob is the one who ended up with twelve sons that became the big jump toward the fulfillment of the promise.

Beginning at Genesis 29:31 and going all the way over to Genesis 30:24 you have the account of the birth of eleven tribes of Israel. Benjamin (number 12) wasn't born until Jacob had returned to his homelands. These verses give us the low points in an intense sibling rivalry between Leah and Rachel, which also included each of their servants (Bilhah and Zilpah), so that Jacob's children came from these four women (Leah had six, Rachel two, Bilhah two, and Zilpah two).

Jacob fathered all these children but was absent as a husband and parent. Other than an angry outburst at Rachel in which he told his wife her infertility was God's fault (Gen. 30:2), Jacob is noticeably missing.

Where is Jacob? Is he at work? Is he on the golf course? Is he on the road? He's the poster guy for failed fatherhood.

Neglect of family among men is epidemic. Husbands and fathers are passive when we should be taking action. We're weak when we should be strong. We're selfish when we should be generous. We're distracted when we should be focused.

There was such a stronghold in the life of Jacob also found in so many men who work so hard at so many things, but not about the things that matter most. We can say and think that we're doing all that we do for our families, but if we were thinking differently, we would see that many of our efforts go on behind the walls of the stronghold of selfishness.

If you're a husband, what are the Jacob-like strongholds in your life?

If you're a wife, what strongholds do you see in the four women in Jacob's household that may echo in your life?

End this assignment with an extended time of prayer for your spouse's struggle with strongholds, and don't neglect asking God for His intervention in your own.

DAY 4
MORE STEPS ON THE BAD COURSE

Yesterday we looked at two of the persistent strongholds in Jacob's life. God gave him glimpses of the problem, but he continued the same way. Today we'll look at two more.

Read Genesis 30:25-31:16.

Beginning in Genesis 30:25 you just read a remarkable account of how Jacob became a wealthy man. Basically, as soon as Joseph is born—the son of promise, the son who would one day deliver this entire family after being sold as a slave into Egypt—Jacob decided it was time to go home. Notice the evidence of a stronghold that has been in the family for generations: Jacob favoritism toward Rachel that will be transferred to Joseph.

It's not wrong to get apart from your parents to establish your own household. This is the basic intention of Genesis 2:24: "Therefore a man shall leave his father and his mother and hold fast to his wife," but an inability to create healthy space between your house and your parents' is evidence of a stronghold, perhaps of control.

Interestingly, when Jacob said that he was leaving, Laban showed up and announced sudden spiritual epiphany. "But Laban said to him, 'If I have found favor in your sight, I have learned by divination that the LORD has blessed me because of you'" (Gen. 30:27). Divination? Just think horoscopes, Ouija boards, psychics, and tarot cards. So Laban went up to someone like a fortuneteller to find out what he should have realized all along (and maybe was unwilling to admit). Things had started getting better when Jacob came.

Laban reveals a level of desperation over a change when he said, "Name your wages, and I will give it" (v. 28).

Then Jacob's stronghold surfaced. Jacob should have said, "My wages are X per year. Because I've been working here for this long, you owe me YX. And when I work for this many more years, you'll owe me YX + YX. Sign here. Or, let's call the attorneys. Let's get this in writing." But Jacob did not do that.

A generous offer from God had kept Jacob negotiating after his dream. Now a broad offer from his father-in-law took him right back to cheating again. Even though Jacob was crushed when he was tricked by Laban substituting Leah for Rachel at his wedding, he would use deception, again, to set off a sheep breeding competition.

Jacob deceived Laban to try to get an advantage. What's remarkable is that God already wanted to bless Jacob. God had promised to take care of Jacob, but Jacob couldn't get out of his own way. Jacob couldn't stop lying even though he had no reason to do it anymore.

By cleverly manipulating the flocks breeding opportunities to produce more of the sheep with markings that would designate them as Jacob's, Jacob gained great wealth and the seething envy of Laban's sons. Things weren't well with Laban either. At this point, the Lord let Jacob know it was time to leave.

Pushed into a corner, Jacob took his wives aside and gave them the big picture. He described for them a scenario in which God and Laban have been in a contest over Jacob, while he's been the innocent party. In Genesis 31:6-7 he told Leah and Rachel, "You know that I have served your father with all my strength, yet your father has cheated me and changed my wages ten times."

Do you remember what we've been learning? Laban has been trying to counter Jacob's moves. What goes around, comes right back on you. Liars get lied to. Cheaters get cheated. I'm not saying that everyone who has had something bad happen to them did something to deserve it; I'm saying that everyone whose life has been about doing bad things to others will experience the same before it's over.

Now what's so amazing is Genesis 31:11-13 where Jacob admitted God has been working behind the scenes all along to bless him, in spite of his shenanigans. God has been trying to take care of Jacob and keep the promises that He has made, but Jacob wasn't willingly let God do it.

What followed was an unexpected show of solidarity between the feuding sisters, justifying Jacob's actions and agreeing it's time to leave—yet another example of God working behind the scenes in ways Jacob doesn't deserve.

Read Genesis 31:17-55 for a view of Jacob's further stronghold of conflict avoidance.

Ironically, three other strongholds we've looked at in Jacob's life—bargaining with God, neglecting his family, and deceiving everyone who crossed his path—are all surefire ways to generate conflict in life. Yet, instead of turning from these patterns, he fled the conflicts he was continually creating. Jacob didn't have to keep avoiding conflict, but he did. We find this pattern of avoidance throughout his life, but the events surrounding his departure from Laban's house provide clear examples.

Like his father and grandfather, Jacob left under cover of darkness and ran from the conflict. That's the way he was. He always deceived. He did what was best for himself, and he couldn't participate in truthful exchanges with others. So Jacob would run and hide.

Although Jacob and his entourage had a two day head start, Laban went after him. When they met up seven days later, the text records a dialogue between liars. Laban had to admit he had been prevented from doing to Jacob what he had planned to do. "It is in my power to do you harm. But the God of your father spoke to me last night, saying, 'Be careful not to say anything to Jacob, either good or bad'" (Gen. 31:29). God protected Jacob even though Jacob was making it so difficult. What Jacob desperately needed was to start thinking differently about God, about himself, about his life, about where blessing comes from, about where consequences come from, and how God rules over all.

The hidden and not-so-hidden costs associated with Jacob's strongholds were high. We can only imagine how things could have been better if he had thought and acted differently. What examples in your life remind you that God often blesses despite our tendencies to function out of our strongholds?

If you haven't been doing so during the week, take a few minutes to pray for each member of your study group, asking the Lord to fill them with courage and strength as they face the strongholds in their lives.

DAY 5
THE MIRROR OF OUR LOVED ONES' LIVES

Like a baton passed from one person to another, the handoff of strongholds between family members and generations, if not resisted, is almost assured. Every generation can be the last one to house a particular stronghold or just another link in the chain of captivity that binds those that come next. The moment any of us witness what we recognize as our stronghold beginning to take hold in a loved one's life is a moment of truth that should drive us to action.

Unfortunately, too many of us have watched strongholds grow up in the behavior of loved ones. Here's my final plea in this week in which we have been looking at the strongholds of our own making: If nothing else scares us into destroying the strongholds in our lives, seeing them in our loved ones should.

Why do you agree or disagree with the plea you just read?

What patterns in your life have you tried to address because you didn't want to see them repeated in your children?

So here it is. Jacob packed up to get out of town, to run away under cover of night. They were leaving and not coming back. And "Rachel stole her father's household gods" (Gen. 31:19). She was leaving her pagan family behind and took what didn't belong to her. How much spiritual impact is Jacob having on his wife that she is willing to leave, but she wants to take their gods? What kind of god do you want that you can put in a suitcase?

Rachel had stolen what she thought might give her father an advantage, but she wasn't alone in practicing deception. She and her husband were a team: "And Jacob tricked Laban" (Gen. 31:20). Then, Rachel also deceived her husband, not telling him she was transporting stolen goods. Stronghold. Stronghold. Stronghold. It hadn't changed yet.

When Laban discovered he had lost his connection to God's blessing as well as the idols he relied upon, he went in hot pursuit of his son-in-law. When he confronted Jacob, the disappearance of the idols was part of the complaint he leveled against Jacob. Since he knew he hadn't taken them, Jacob made the dangerous assumption that the idols weren't in the camp. Surely no one in his family would have been foolhardy enough to commit the theft. So, he gave Laban the right to search the tents and belongings. He even pledged death to anyone discovered with the idols. Imagine how Rachel felt.

> **How well do you identify with Rachel? Have you ever watched your bad choices unravel as others unknowingly put your dishonest or deceitful plan in danger?**

> **When have you seen God prevent you from getting away with something? How have you responded?**

Laban searched the entire camp. He went into his own daughter's tent, muttering, "I'm going to find my idols. Someone's got them. They're my gods, and I need them."

When he saw Rachel sitting on a camel saddle in which she has hidden the idols, Laban said, "Get up. I have to search for my idols."

And Rachel said to her irate father, "'Let not my lord be angry that I cannot rise before you, for the way of women is upon me.' So he searched but did not find the household gods" (v. 35). Rachel was born to a liar. Rachel was married to a liar. What has she become? A liar. Do you see how the strongholds spread? The younger daughter lied to her father's face. The handoff of dishonesty was complete.

We are never told if Rachel ever confessed to her husband what she had done. Somehow, we doubt it. Those household idols Rachel stole are never mentioned again. Later, Jacob returned to Bethel where God met him before his travels. Then he instructed his family, "Put away the foreign gods that are among you and purify yourselves and change your garments" (Gen. 35:2). Perhaps at this point, if not earlier, Rachel got rid of those foolish idols. She certainly had no use for them and had treated them with disdain. Her motivation for stealing them had most likely been to spite her father.

Let me say it again: If nothing else scares us into destroying the strongholds in our lives, seeing them in our loved ones should.

But even as I think about what I just wrote I realize that too many of us are just like the father in Harry Chapin's famous song "Cat's in the Cradle." In the lyrics we listen as a dad reviews all the opportunities he had to make a positive impact in his son's life, but each time he had a pressing excuse, a stronghold of other priorities. And, each time, his son says, "I'm going to grow up just like you, Dad." When the father finally gets around to suggesting he and the boy spend some time together, the roles are suddenly reversed, because now the son is just too busy. He has in fact grown up to be just like his dad.

If we don't make the hard decisions to think differently, Harry Chapin's story—in so many hurtful, destructive ways—could be our kids' stories and our grandkids' stories. The strongholds have now been detected. We know where they have come from and we know they are not going away without a fight. We may not yet know how to think differently, but we are reaching that place where we will not be content until we are thinking differently. The next time we're together, we're going to be working on destroying strongholds.

> **End by praying for the people most directly affected by the strongholds in your life. Realize that at some point along the way, when you are thinking differently, you may need to approach some of them to confess that you have passed on to them some stronghold that you trust they will ask God to help them demolish.**

> **Ask God for wisdom and a willing heart as we move into the major demolition part of the study.**

WHEN STRONGHOLDS START TO CRUMBLE

Welcome to week 7 of Think Differently.

After opening the group time in prayer, give anyone who would like to share a "thinking differently" experience from the last week an opportunity to speak. If this takes quite a bit of time, you may want to just move into the DVD teaching for this session. Otherwise choose any of the following questions to prepare for the lesson.

For parents in the group: Describe one thing (hopefully funny) that one of your kids does just like you, or even like your parents.

What are some ways you are praying differently for your family since this study began?

In what ways has this study turned out different than what you expected at the beginning?

We've been learning to think about our thinking because our thinking influences everything we do. If what we are doing bothers us, the only way we're really going to change is by changing our thinking. We're looking for the ways God has given us to change our minds.

This session is "When Strongholds Start to Crumble." What have you seen already in your life to indicate one or more strongholds are crumbling?

To prepare for the teaching, read together the following verses:

For though we walk in the flesh, we are not waging war according to the flesh. For the weapons of our warfare are not of the flesh but have divine power to destroy strongholds. We destroy arguments and every lofty opinion raised against the knowledge of God, and take every thought captive to obey Christ, being ready to punish every disobedience, when your obedience is complete.
2 CORINTHIANS 10:3-6

WATCH

COMPLETE THE VIEWER GUIDE BELOW AS YOU WATCH DVD SESSION 7.

Strongholds start to crumble when the consequences reach a _____ point.

Eventually you get to the place in your life where God lets you feel the _____ _____ of the choices that you have been making.

Five Strongest Strongholds:

1. Self-_____.
2. Self-_____.
3. Self-_____.
4. Self-_____.
5. Self-_____.

Strongholds start to crumble when you finally get _____ alone.

When we get alone:

1. _____cease
2. _____ end
3. _____ invades
4. _____ starts
5. _____ speaks

Strongholds start to crumble when God _____ with you.

Strongholds start to crumble when God _____ over you physically.

Strongholds start to crumble when God _____ you forever spiritually.

DISCUSS THE DVD SEGMENT WITH YOUR GROUP, USING THE QUESTIONS BELOW.

We've had seven sessions of watching the life of Jacob unfold. What is your impression of Jacob? What would you do if he was moving next door to you?

James described five wrecking balls that can shake strongholds into crumbling: crisis points, time alone, contending with God, getting beaten by God, and being marked by God. Which one of these have you witnessed in someone else? What were the results?

Which stronghold crumblers have you experienced firsthand?

God orchestrates any or all of these. How do they make you feel about Him?

Which of these do you hope you never have to experience or experience again? Why?

In reviewing the five things that can happen when we get alone (demands cease, distractions end, quiet invades, reflection starts, and God speaks), how many of these do you know firsthand are true? Which ones promote the most change in you?

Application: Of the actions on Jacob's part that we saw in this session, deciding to be alone was the one choice that set in motion God's painful but necessary work of undermining Jacob's strongholds. Scheduling time alone this week could have the same beneficial effect in your life. As you close, take a few minutes as a group to pray for each other, asking for God's help in making strongholds crumble.

This week's Scripture memory passage:

> *Come now, let us reason together, says the LORD: though your sins are like scarlet, they shall be as white as snow; though they are red like crimson, they shall become like wool. If you are willing and obedient, you shall eat the good of the land; but if you refuse and rebel, you shall be eaten by the sword; for the mouth of the LORD has spoken.*
> **ISAIAH 1:18-20**

Assignment: Complete the daily lessons for this next week in preparation for the next group experience. Set aside several hours to be alone with God, tracking the five things that can happen when we're alone that James mentioned in the session. Continue the practice of praying for each of your group by name, asking God to help them think differently this week.

WHEN STRONGHOLDS START TO CRUMBLE

Something has to give. We've been studying the life of Jacob and we have learned that nothing is different until we think differently, that all change begins with a change of mind. We've realized what strongholds are fortified patterns of thinking in our lives that are stubbornly resistant to God's Word and to God's will. If you've been trying to go forward and you can't, or if you're stuck and you can't get traction, the biblical term for that is a stronghold.

Some of our strongholds come from our disposition. Some of our strongholds come from our family dysfunction, and we all have some of that. But a good bit of it comes from our own decisions and personal patterns. Change isn't coming until we let God destroy our strongholds and arguments and lofty opinions (2 Cor. 10:3-6) that have raised themselves, or exalted themselves, against the knowledge of God. Our goal is to take every thought captive to the obedience of Christ for our greater joy which brings God greater glory.

This week we are again observing the life of Jacob and the way God worked to begin demolishing his strongholds. The destruction of arguments and lofty opinions is necessary but can be a painful process. It certainly was for Jacob.

DAY 1
WHEN GOD CREATES CRISIS

Read Genesis 32:1-22.

Eventually you get to the place in your life where God lets you feel the full weight of the choices that you have been making. There's grace in that place. There's mercy. But that is also the place where our God of steadfast love lets us feel the full weight of all the garbage that we have created by not trusting Him. When all that junk comes crashing down, that's God trying to get our attention. You've just read an account of an escalating crisis in Jacob's life.

At this point in the story, Jacob must have been thinking, *It didn't have to come to this. It didn't have to be this way.* When all of the consequences of bad choices come crashing down upon us, as they did on Jacob, it can be the beginning of the end for a stronghold. Something wonderful is on the other side. Strongholds begin to crumble when the consequences reach a crisis point.

Genesis 32:22 describes Jacob's desperate actions. "The same night he arose and took his two wives, his two female servants, [these are the mothers of his children] and his eleven children, and crossed the ford of the Jabbok."

In some places the water of the Jabbok runs very strongly. It would have been up to at least to his waist, if not higher. It was quite an effort to move this large family, their luggage, and all of the animals that remained. He got them all across the river because he was at a crisis point, dreading his encounter with Esau. But facing all the consequences of his youth, even though he's old, brings back the realities of his past. As I often say, "You're only young once, but you can be immature for life." Just because you have reached middle-age in years doesn't mean you're still not a selfish little boy or girl in many ways. Immaturity can contain a lot of strongholds. There has to be a real change in order to grow up. Coming to church or sitting through small group doesn't fix it. We have to allow God to bring an ax to bear on the trunk of our strongholds, to launch a grenade into the fortification that we have raised against the knowledge of God.

In what ways has your participation in this study created any crises in you?

It grieves me to think that we've gone through everything we've gone through in these weeks and there are still probably those who are still allowing themselves the luxury of staying kind of vague about the reality of strongholds in their lives.

If you fit that category, you still don't have anything specific in mind as a stronghold. As I've tried to lay out in a detailed, careful way, you've listened and maybe even agreed, but you haven't personally taken hold of two or three things that you're praying and asking God to change about you. So you are bound up in lust, consumed with having and acquiring, or some other fortified thinking we've talked about. Or, you do not belong to Jesus the way that you want to because you belong to your own efforts to make your life secure. Whatever that idol is, you're holding on to it still.

The part of you that realizes you have strongholds is the part of you that is under attack by the enemy to remain silent. The tactics he uses are obvious but effective. The enemy always condemns us with generalities in order to keep us from calling out to God. Under his suggestion we end up thinking, *I am awful. I have horrendous strongholds. I am sure I do. I'm sure they're shameful and make me completely unworthy of God's care.*

That thinking is not from the Lord. God loves us, and He is so specific with us. The Bible says that love is patient (1 Cor. 13:4). God waits for us to recognize the particular problems so we can see the changes He can bring about. He convicts us about specifics. He wants us to get beyond general superficialities to the deeper matters of thinking differently. He wants to replace our muddled mind with the mind of Christ.

Why is it important to remember that Satan condemns with generalities while God convicts with specifics? Consider this thought: generalities immobilize while specifics motivate.

For those who have any doubts, let me mention another list of the five strongest strongholds. If you haven't taken hold of something that you want destroyed in your life, get one of these. Here they are:

- **Self-righteousness.** This is the stronghold that declares, "I don't need God's forgiveness. I don't need to be saved. I don't need a Savior. I'll be fine. I'm a good person." Or in the life of a believer, "I needed His forgiveness once, but I don't need it anymore."

Self-righteousness is that pattern of thinking that causes you to consistently look at others and consider yourself superior. But God's Word says that we should "count others more significant than yourselves" (Phil. 2:3). If you esteem yourself better than others, that's self-righteousness and pride. Self-righteousness is death to god-liness and death to fellowship. Is self-righteousness a stronghold in your life?

- **Self-deception.** This stronghold says, "I just don't hear God speak. I come to church, listen to the preacher, but he's just a guy talking. God's Word is not the authority over my life. I don't hear it as though God were speaking to me. I'm unaware that God is dealing with me or that He is confronting me.

You have a significant stronghold in your life where you just don't let the Lord speak to you—not just at church, but on your own. You don't have extended times with the Lord where He's getting your attention and redirecting your life. That is a massive stronghold.

- **Self-loathing.** Do you find yourself saying, "I don't believe God loves me. I don't feel worthy of God's love?" The truth is we're not! But this stronghold believes that love is only gained through worthiness, that love can only be earned. What has to die is your sense of unworthiness for God's love, for we are all unworthy. What has to die is your sense that love can only come when it's earned. The gospel doesn't just proclaim our unworthiness; it is also a significant message you need to hear about how great the love of God is for you. I believe that both need to be taught. If you have a stronghold of self-loathing, that love of God part of the message might not be coming through to you. God would love to tear that down.

- **Self-centeredness.** "I don't seek God's will. I am the master of my fate. I am the captain of my soul." You don't seek God when you're making a decision. Instead of praying and pondering, you just kind of choose and act. That's what you've always done. Self-centeredness is a big stronghold. It's not seeking counsel and living in submission to the Lord as Christians are commanded and motivated by love to do. Self-centeredness says, "I do what's best for me. I don't care who it hurts.

- **Self-confidence.** "I don't want God's help. I want to get it done myself. There's only I in my team. It really is all about me. I'm the one who wins and gets it done. I achieve and don't share the spotlight with anyone." Believing in self is a thinly veiled stronghold.

I really would rather never go through that self-strongholds list again, but I just hate the thought that we would go forward into all the good that's waiting for us in the weeks ahead if you were still being held back because you are blind to any specific threshold you may have.

> **Whether it's from the list above or a previous discovery, what's a specific stronghold or two in your life that you are bringing before God in the sessions to come?**

> **End your homework for today with a prayer of thanksgiving to God for the crises He has allowed into your life, even those that have been very difficult.**

DAY 2
THE EFFECTIVE CRISIS OF TIME ALONE

When we left Jacob yesterday in Genesis 32:22-23, he had just transported his family across the Jabbok River. Look at the beginning of Genesis 32:24, "And Jacob was left alone." This is key because God is about to confront Jacob, and yet God doesn't confront us very often most deeply until we are by ourselves. My hope and prayer for today is that you will take whatever steps are needed this week to get some extended, structured time alone with your Bible open and with a pen and a journal beside you. And then, that you're going to invite God to confront you with truth and deliverance.

When was the last time God took you to the mat with the full weight of who He is? When? A month ago? A year ago? The truth may be that you haven't put a tear on an altar or had a meaningful extended time of prayer with God in years. When is that going to change? If it isn't going to change during a series like this, it may never happen.

> **How does this last paragraph apply to your life? What was your specific answer to the questions?**

When we get alone we put ourselves in a special place. Here's what can happen when we get alone:

- **Demands cease.** No generation—no civilization—has ever had the burdens on it that you and I have today. The demands on us are unbelievable. The career expectations, economic anxieties, demands of marriage and parenting are confusing and crushing. There's just an immense pressure in society in general to know, participate, and be involved. There really isn't enough time in a day to do all the things that need to be done. Someone coined the phrase "tyranny of the urgent" to describe our frantic pace. We never calendar an appointment that says, "Stop all of that and get alone with God for an extended period of time where you won't be interrupted."

Getting alone means disconnecting so, for awhile, demands go unanswered—so a deeper need can be addressed.

- **Distractions end.** As long as your smartphone is in your hand or in sight, you won't be alone. The constant ringing of calls, dinging of messages, and all the different tones connected with our social media accounts leave us in a continual state of distraction.

The amount of time that goes into distraction demands a price we pay in terms of intimate relationship with our Creator, who can take us and shake us when we need it—and we do need it. But when we get alone, demands cease and distraction ends.

- **Quiet invades.** For many of us, the experience may be profoundly unsettling but healthy. When was the last time you were quiet and able to do nothing with that time but think?

My phone is off; it's in the other room. My home is empty and will be for several hours. The television is not on. I'm not piping music into my ears. It's quiet, but I'm not going to take a nap. I'm going to sit at the kitchen table with my Bible open. I'm going to ask God to make His Word a mirror to me as He says it is. And I want to see myself. I want Him to challenge me, to confront me, to contend with me. I want God to demolish these strongholds of my needs to be busy, to feel happy, to have everything perfect, to have "enough" money, and to eat whatever I want—to be happy.

It takes a quiet place and time to be able to actually pray, "God, I'm begging You to come and contend with me, and tear these strongholds down."

- **Reflection starts.** Socrates said, "The unexamined life is not worth living." That's quite a statement. The life that does not reflect upon itself is reflecting in vain. It's remarkable to me how many believers have a long list of what needs fixing in others. But what is God's view of me? In the end, that's all that's going to matter. Yes, He loves me, and He has forgiven me in Christ, but that surely does not mean that He is content for me to remain as I am.

- **God speaks**. C. S. Lewis made the point that God often whispers to us in our pleasures, and His voice is amplified in our pains. Lewis could have also reminded us that God doesn't try to outshout our noise, demands, and distractions. He can interrupt non-verbally in very effective ways, but when God speaks, most often it's when we're quiet.

Which of the five byproducts of alone time is most appealing to you? Why?

How many of them would be unfamiliar or even frightening territory for you?

Again I ask, when was the last time you asked God to take you to the mat with the full weight of who He is? It's awesome. I thankfully can say very recently, and I want you to join me there. Do it soon and do it often.

I realize that sometimes we don't get alone with God because we sense that He is going to say something that we don't want to hear. That is such a poor choice because it keeps us from getting all the good that God always has for us, even when it has to arrive through pain.

For today and this moment, I'm asking you to choose some time alone with God. Do it this week.

Before you close this workbook for today, decide when you will make some time alone with God this week. Share your plan with someone else in the study group and ask them to hold you accountable for following through. You might even consider leaving your phone and other distractions in their care while you embark on your encounter with God.

GOING TOE TO TOE WITH GOD

Yesterday we spent our time thinking about the first phrase in Genesis 32:24, "And Jacob was left alone." Today we will consider that Jacob wasn't alone for long. The verse goes on to say, "And a man wrestled with him until the breaking of the day." Perhaps you've already discovered that God isn't on our schedule. Being alone with Him doesn't go well if our attitude is, "I've got about fifteen minutes to squeeze you in, Lord. What do you have for me today?" We're not told what Jacob was expecting when he was alone, but God didn't disappoint Jacob. He discovered firsthand what the New Testament promises, "Draw near to God and he will draw near to you" (Jas. 4:8).

> **During times in your life when you have been alone with God to "draw near to Him," what are some of the different ways He has drawn near to you?**

> **How have some of these daily homework assignments been wrestling with God for you?**

The strongholds in Jacob's life began to crumble when God contended with him personally. That's what God Himself began to do; He wrestled with Jacob. The match lasted all night. It's useful for us to remember that this entire contest was conducted during hours of darkness. Jacob never saw his opponent. This was hand-to-hand combat during which Jacob must have been struggling for his life. During the fight, our flawed hero realized he wasn't fighting just another human, but God.

At this point you may be thinking, *Well, Pastor James, forgive me for saying so, but you keep referring to this wrestling match as between Jacob and God. And the Word of God clearly says that it's a man. I expect more careful study from you than that.*

First of all, thank you for your attention to what the text actually says. Let's look closely at a bit more of the story.

Note that the word translated *man* is the Hebrew word *ish* (pronounced eesh), which could be translated "warrior." This is a warrior that has come to wrestle with Jacob. Jacob got into the fight ring by getting himself alone, but God started the actual struggle. Imagine Jacob standing by the river alone in the black of night one minute and then suddenly feeling strong hands on him the next. Spurred on by fear or stubbornness, Jacob didn't go down and give up. He locked up with his opponent, and the match apparently went on for hours, eventually dragging into a stalemate.

What would you say is the importance of identifying Jacob's opponent in the fight as God Himself?

At this point we get our first clear indication that the "warrior" isn't just a man who picked a fight with Jacob: "When the man saw that he did not prevail against Jacob, he touched his hip socket" (Gen. 32:25).

The hip socket is probably the strongest joint in the body. To get your hip socket out of joint, it takes two very strong opposing forces—such as your body and the impact of a car accident or a long fall. Hip dislocation is one of the most painful injuries that a human being can experience.

In high school I got my knuckle out of joint playing football. I was blocking a guy and got my finger in the way when our helmets collided. I mean, there is no way that hurt less than having a fork stuck in my eye. My finger is still crooked. That hurt!

Here the wrestler touched Jacob's hip and out popped the ball joint. No twisting or leverage, just a touch to work a painful miracle. This is one of the clear indications that Jacob's opponent is God because human beings don't do miracles: "He touched his hip socket, and Jacob's hip was put out of joint as he wrestled with Him. Then he said, 'Let me go, for the day has broken'" (Genesis 32:25-26).

Dislocated hip and all, Jacob still wouldn't tap out. He said, "I will not let you go unless you bless me" (v. 26). Again, why would Jacob make his request if he didn't realize at this point that he's been wrestling with God? Blessing is ultimately the prerogative of deity. You don't ask a stranger, especially if you've been wrestling with him all night, to bless you. The request assumes Jacob knows he's holding on to someone capable of blessing him.

How important are God's blessing in your life?

What are some of them? Which ones did you ask for specifically and which ones has He graciously given without you asking?

The man's response to Jacob is significant in two ways and confirms the warrior's identity. First, "And he said to him, 'What is your name?' And he said, 'Jacob'" (Gen. 32:27). So if this is just a man, this is some man because He is changing Jacob's name in the next verse.

People don't do that to other people, but God could certainly claim the right to give you a new name. And the second and most compelling reason comes in the explanation of the patriarch's new name: "Then he said, 'Your name shall no longer be called Jacob, but Israel, for you have striven with God'" (Gen. 32:28).

Who is Jacob striving with? God! Who's confronting him? God! Who's contending with him? God! Jacob got a new name after grappling all night with God.

The encounter by Jabbok was never about Jacob getting alone and figuring a few things out on his own. It was about God contending with Jacob in grace, love, sweat, and pain to create in Jacob a different way of thinking.

It's true that nothing is really going to be different in your life, as it was in Jacob's, until you begin to think differently. It's also true that you won't begin to really think differently until you realize how much God wants to be a part in making it happen for you.

Take a few minutes again to pray for your fellow study group members, asking God to graciously wrestle with them this week.

Thank God for showing up and confronting you at various times in your life, whether you thought you needed Him or not.

DAY 4
WHEN GOD TAKES YOU TO THE MAT

Can we agree that the wrestling match we saw yesterday was a pretty unique way to experience interaction with God?

So, if the fight lasted for hours, how hard was God trying? Jacob had to be thinking, *This is a joke; I'm wrestling with God!* And yet he was so invested in the struggle that he wouldn't give up. He couldn't win, but he didn't quit either—not until God took him to the mat.

The moment by the river between Jacob and God invites us to flash forward to a stretch of road between Jerusalem and Damascus where a man named Saul was laid out in the dust by God. As Saul, by then called Paul, remembered the encounter, it wasn't much of a fight: "At midday, O king, I saw on the way a light from heaven, brighter than the sun, that shone around me and those who journeyed with me. And when we had all fallen to the ground, I heard a voice saying to me in the Hebrew language, 'Saul, Saul, why are you persecuting me? It is hard for you to kick against the goads.' And I said, 'Who are you, Lord?' And the Lord said, 'I am Jesus whom you are persecuting'" (Acts 26:13-15). When the time is right, at midnight or high noon, God will contend with you.

Examples like these and many others in Scripture remind us that God's dealing with us has a lot to do with our dispositions. God knows every detail of the way He designed us as well as every twist and bend that has inflicted on His design by sin, by environment, by our families, and by our own decisions. He knows what it will take to get us to the moments of decision. He knows what it will take to bring us to that place where we see the necessity of thinking differently.

Some of us have a flawed disposition like stone that has to be shattered. Others have towering pride like a massive tree that has to be cut down. Some of us are wounded and weakened sheep that the Shepherd gently tends. You and I are wasting time if we insist on knowing why God laid us out in what seems like a harder way than someone else: "God, why didn't you slam him to the mat like you did me? Why did I have to stumble and land on my face when she skipped through the same stuff and never missed a step?" We already know the answer. God always handles us the exactly the way we need to be handled, whether we like it or not.

In what ways has God used physical means in your life as part of His strategy in drawing you to Him?

What are some examples of God "taking you to the mat" easily or hard over strongholds in your life?

God is so gentle, right? Why did He fight Jacob that way? Why didn't He just pin Jacob and make him tap out? Because He's gentle and because He knows Jacob like no one else could ever knew him. To the scratching, clawing, and striving Jacob, God wanted to say what Jesus said to all of us, "Come to me, all who labor and are heavy laden, and I will give you rest. Take my yoke upon you, and learn from me, for I am gentle and lowly in heart, and you will find rest for your souls" (Matt. 11:28-29).

When you think about God's gentleness, what personal experiences come to mind?

After all of these years and countless examples of strongholds in Jacob's life, none of us would say that God was over the top or off base if He was finally impatient with Jacob. Just as He wouldn't be out of line to bring the hammer down on me, or you, but He is so gentle and so persistent. God's patience with us should make us appreciate His patience with others. It should compel us toward greater patience with one another.

God wasn't in a hurry to finish His match with Jacob. God had a purpose in the fight and its conclusion. He knew what He was doing. In everything that happened, God had a much bigger picture in mind than just that match. That night beside the Jabbok River, God was also thinking of us. "Now these things happened to them as an example, but they were written down for our instruction, on whom the end of the ages has come" (1 Corinthians 10:11). God wanted us to see Him contend with Jacob before He showed us a resolution and demolition of his strongholds. He longs for us to know He will participate in the ugly and entrenched places in our lives to set us free.

That's what's going to happen right here: "When the man saw that he did not prevail against Jacob, he touched his hip socket, and Jacob's hip was put out of joint as he wrestled with him" (Gen. 32:25). God didn't exercise His divine prerogative until the time was right. Just before dawn, God concluded that this guy wasn't going to let it go. He was not going to give up.

Jacob was fighting to have his way right until the end. And the Lord just touched him, and the fight was over. Jacob was left hanging on so he wouldn't fall down.

God's actions communicated, "It didn't have to be this way, Jacob. You could've submitted. You could've lain down; I didn't have to put you down. But you're insisting on this pain. You're insisting on this outcome. Do you really want it this way?"

As we imagine Jacob grunting and writhing in pain we need to understand that God would rather see you and me crushed than living with a stronghold. He would rather see us in a hospital bed than living with a stronghold. And God would rather see me broken and alone with the weight of all of the dumb choices I've made crashing down on top of me than to stand back passively and let me go on the way that I am.

Would you say your pattern of struggle with God has been more marked by gentle reminders or rough confrontations when you realized again who was in charge?

How do you explain His tactics with you?

God comes to us when we're alone, and He contends with us—but He always prevails. He does what is necessary to finally get our attention. And the underlying tone of sadness from the Lord will often be, "It didn't have to be this way."

"Then he said, 'Let me go, for the day has broken.' But Jacob said, 'I will not let you go unless you bless me.' And he said to him, 'What is your name?'" (Genesis 32:26-27). There was no question that Jacob would be letting go. The only real question was, "How much will he learn and change this time?"

Have you just realized that you've been struggling against God for a long time in ways that were unnecessary? What has that wrestling looked like?

In what areas do those struggles usually take place?

What would it take for you to surrender?

End your homework time by telling God how you see His work in your life, particularly the places where He has had to come at you hard to stop you in your tracks. Thank Him for being willing to risk His relationship with you by loving you enough to contend with you.

DAY 5
SCARS TO CHERISH

The whole point of this week has been to realize that some strongholds in our lives will not begin to crumble until God wrestles with us and demonstrates who's really in charge. And sometimes we don't really start to think differently until God marks us forever spiritually.

Read Genesis 32:26-32 again.

Jacob's hip had been dislocated and the fight was almost over. God responded in an unexpected way to Jacob's grunted request for a blessing in exchange for letting go: "And He said to him, 'What is your name?'" (v.27). Did the Lord know his name? Of course. So why did He ask Jacob?

You have to understand that naming kids is not the same as now. We have three children and each of their names comes with a story, but it's frankly not very spiritual or even awe inspiring. The names we give our kids today are usually connected with cultural popularity, family history, and sometimes quirky personal preferences.

That's not the way naming came about in the Bible. In biblical times, you often got a name that was positive because your parents hoped and prayed that you could live up to it, or you got a name that was negative because, above all things, it represented a stronghold they wanted you to avoid. The name, "Jacob" means supplanter, heel-catcher, or cheater. Remember how the birth of the twins was described? "The first came out red, all his body like a hairy cloak, so they called his name Esau. Afterward his brother came out with his hand holding Esau's heel, so his name was called Jacob" (Gen. 25:25-26). Events connected with their birth helped determine the names of both brothers.

The Lord asked Jacob as he was on the ground in pain, "What's your name?"

When Jacob uttered his name out loud he was basically saying, "My name is liar. I lie. I grasp and connive. It's what I do. It's what I've always done."

Here's the whole exchange: "And he said to him, 'What is your name?' And he said, 'Jacob.' Then he said, 'Your name shall no longer be called Jacob, but Israel, for you have striven with God and with men, and have prevailed'" (Gen. 32:27-28).

First, Jesus canceled the old name. He was essentially saying, "Lying and grasping? You may have been that, but you're not going to be that anymore. You may have done that, but you're not going to do that anymore. You won't excuse it. You won't defend it. If you struggle with it, you'll forsake it immediately. You will never live and lounge and languish in that sin anymore."

God won the fight, but Isaac's son got the blessing of a new name. We could say, "Jacob, you wrestled with God and came out a winner. Israel, the name of a nation, is your new name."

"Then Jacob asked him, 'Please tell me your name'" (v. 29). When Jacob expressed his curiosity, God answered, "'Why is it that you ask my name?' And there He blessed him" (v. 29).

It wasn't, "It's about time this stronghold came down!" No. Jacob had no answer for Jesus' response, but after what must have been an awkward silence, the text tells us Jesus "blessed him." Jacob's question didn't need an answer because Jacob already knew who had wrestled, defeated, and then blessed him: "So Jacob called the name of the place Peniel, saying, 'For I have seen God face to face, and yet my life has been delivered'" (Gen. 32:30).

When you look back over your life, what scars and dislocations can you see that God has caused in order to get you serious about Him?

How did meeting God personally cause a significant change in your life?

Everything is changing here. Jacob was not going to be the same. "The sun rose upon him as he passed Penuel, limping because of his hip" (v. 31). So, for the rest of this Jacob's life, he was limping with every step and reminded every time he heard his name, "I wrestled with God and won—even though He beat me. I'm not a liar anymore. That stronghold has been destroyed." He was changed.

As we end this week, I'm challenging you to wrestle with God about some things that have been weighing you down or simply hiding in the background as you have traveled through these sessions. It's time to stop letting your stronghold(s) define you. I trust you've found time to be alone this week and have experienced God contending with you. You may even be limping emotionally or in some other way as a result. I'm challenging you to yield to God, to let Him prevail, to be marked for the rest of your life.

If not now, when are you going to settle things with God? He loves you so deeply that no stronghold is safe enough to keep you from Him. He will demolish the barriers if you will let Him.

If you're wondering to yourself, *Okay, I see what God does about strongholds, but what can I do? What's my role in moving toward thinking differently?*

The answer to that question is, "I repent." In the New Testament, the word repentance is *metanoia.* The word actually means a change of mind. If repentance was easy everyone would be doing it. We're going to be studying repentance in the next part of this series because we need time to understand its depth. Repentance is a wonderful thing. It's nothing to be shunned; it is something to be run to. Everything good happens after genuine repentance. It literally means "changing your mind."

The Bible says that God grants repentance. As you meet with Him alone and uninterrupted, ask God to grant you repentance about things He wants to change.

> **Take a few minutes to pray for the others in your study group, asking for them what you are asking God for yourself, a life that is open to the changes He wants to bring about.**

> **Sit quietly in God's presence for at least fifteen minutes. Expect His Spirit to speak to you in that silence.**

REPENTANCE BREAKS STRONGHOLDS

Welcome back to week eight of this study of Think Differently.

During this series we've gotten used to idea that "Nothing is different until you think differently." One of the direct corollaries of this thought is the reality that a big part of thinking differently is praying differently. Have two or three volunteers open the time in prayer for the group.

Use the following questions to expand the discussion while encouraging everyone to participate.

How has your prayer life been affected or change by this study?

What stronghold crumbling stories do you have to share as we prepare for this session's teaching?

At this point in the study we are moving from recognizing strongholds to becoming resolute about seeing them demolished. One of the tendencies shared by every temperament we represent is our default strategy of solving problems on our own. We know we're thinking differently when our first thought is to turn to God rather than our own resources. That's where we find ourselves in this session.

To prepare for the teaching in this session, read together the following verses:

> *For even if I made you grieve with my letter, I do not regret it—though I did regret it, for I see that that letter grieved you, though only for a while. As it is, I rejoice, not because you were grieved, but because you were grieved into repenting. For you felt a godly grief, so that you suffered no loss through us. For godly grief produces a repentance that leads to salvation without regret, whereas worldly grief produces death. For see what earnestness this godly grief has produced in you, but also what eagerness to clear yourselves, what indignation, what fear, what longing, what zeal, what punishment! At every point you have proved yourselves innocent in the matter.*
> **2 CORINTHIANS 7:8-11**

WATCH

COMPLETE THE VIEWER GUIDE BELOW AS YOU WATCH DVD SESSION 8.

Some things we _____ think differently about; some things we _____ think differently about.

Strongholds: Those _____ patterns of thinking that are stubbornly resistant to God's _____ and God's _____ for us.

I'm not what I _____ be; I'm not what I _____ be, but I'm not what I _____.

The most frequently used word in the Old and New Testament for this matter of changing your thinking and changing your mind is the Greek word *metanoia*, which means _____.

Repentance is not a place we _____; repentance is where we _____.

Repentance brings _____.

Repentance is a really _____ thing.

Only _____ can bring you to the place of genuine repentance.

Repentance: A _____ of sin, followed by _____ sorrow, culminating in a change of _____.

Five Marks of Genuine Repentance:

1. _____ over sin.
2. _____ toward sin.
3. _____ toward others
4. _____ toward God
5. A _____ focus

RESPOND

DISCUSS THE DVD SEGMENT WITH YOUR GROUP, USING THE QUESTIONS BELOW.

Listening to that review of the changes in Jacob, what did you find encouraging?

Just before the teaching we talked a little about repentance. How have the last few minutes clarified or deepened your understanding of repentance?

Why is repentance a good thing? Why is it crucial to know that only God can bring you to real repentance?

James described five steps of authentic repentance. Mention each one and explain how you understand it. Which one is the most difficult for you? Why?

Matthew 3:8 says, "Bear fruit in keeping with repentance." What is your response to the challenge that Christians should live in repentance daily?

How does repentance break strongholds?

Based on this session's teaching, which of the three common strongholds (pride, pleasure, priorities) is currently the biggest thing interfering with your relationship with Christ?

Application: James made it clear that we can't schedule or take a rain-check on repentance. It's a crisis that God initiates, that we either respond to or reject. How has God brought you to places of repentance throughout these sessions?

Take a few minutes with the group to pray with each other asking for God's help responding with repentance when God brings awareness of strongholds.

This week's Scripture memory. Let's keep working on the series theme verses:

> *For though we walk in the flesh, we are not waging war according to the flesh. For the weapons of our warfare are not of the flesh but have divine power to destroy strongholds. We destroy arguments and every lofty opinion raised against the knowledge of God, and take every thought captive to obey Christ, being ready to punish every disobedience, when your obedience is complete.* **2 CORINTHIANS 10:3-6**

Assignment: Complete the daily lessons for this next week in preparation for the next group experience. Ask yourself each day: *How have I lived in repentance today?* Make a note of further questions or thoughts related to this week's teaching that you can share with other group members. Pray for each of your group by name, asking God to help them think differently this week.

REPENTANCE BREAKS STRONGHOLDS

Christians aren't very good at changing their minds. In fact, we're probably the worst segment of society because we have things that we are convicted about because we have things that we must hold on to and because we have things that cannot change. As Christians, we hold some truths to be absolute. It starts with our rock solid understanding of who God is, the character and divinity of Jesus Christ, what He did for us on the cross, and the foundation of God's trustworthy Word that informs and guides our lives. In a world that flaunts its disdain for absolutes, and in which everything is up for grabs, we can sometimes appear to be close-minded. But that's not it; we're simply certain about some things and will not be changing our minds about them any time soon.

Now, it's very easy for that kind of determined thinking to drift over into areas that not only can change but need to change and must change. Some things we cannot think differently about. Quite a few things we must think differently about.

All this week we are working on what it means to live in repentance. When it comes to repentance, we sometimes have to repent that we have been unwilling to change our minds, and at other times repentance flows because we have changed our minds where we should have remained steadfast. Face it, if thinking differently were simple and painless, everybody would be doing it!

DAY 1
CHANGING ON GOD'S TIMETABLE

As we've gone through the life of Jacob, we've talked a lot about Jacob's strong-holds—those fortified patterns of thinking that are stubbornly resistant to God's Word and God's will for us. But look at Genesis 28:6. Isaac had just told Jacob that he's going to have a long journey to find the wife. Isaac doesn't want Jacob to be like his brother Esau.

> Now Esau saw that Isaac had blessed Jacob and sent him away to Paddan-aram to take a wife from there, and that as he blessed him he directed him, "You must not take a wife from the Canaanite women," and that Jacob had obeyed his father and his mother and gone to Paddan-aram. So when Esau saw that the Canaanite women did not please Isaac his father, Esau went to Ishmael and took as his wife, besides the wives he had, Mahalath the daughter of Ishmael, Abraham's son, the sister of Nebaioth.
> **GENESIS 28:6-9**

Jacob obeyed his father while Esau basically, in a different way, made the same mistake again. So you have two brothers here, both with a lot of strongholds, both have a lot of room to grow (just like you and me). But the road is starting to fork.

We make life-changing decisions every day, but some prove to be more obvious and impactful as time goes on. Looking back on your life, what have been two or three of the most significant forks in the road, where the choice you made has made a big difference?

It's interesting that in Malachi 1:2-3, God says, "'I have loved you,' says the LORD. But you say, 'How have you loved us?' 'Is not Esau Jacob's brother?' declares the LORD.. 'Yet I have loved Jacob but Esau I have hated." And in Romans 9:13 the statement is confirmed: "As it is written, 'Jacob I loved, but Esau I hated.'"

These are strong words for us to accept. What is it about these two men that God so despises the character of one? Without question, God has sovereignly chosen to place His favor upon Jacob. And yet, already the fingerprint of that favor is showing up in his conduct. Here Jacob changes direction and breaks with the pattern of his brother, submits himself to the counsel of his father, no doubt planning to take a local wife or his father wouldn't have said, "Don't do that; do this." But because Jacob's father said it, he changed his mind and didn't do what he was intending to do. Jacob did something different.

Considering the instances of significant decisions in your life above, take a moment to express gratitude to God for either blessing a good decision or preserving you despite a poor one.

Now look at Genesis 28:16, "Then Jacob awoke from his sleep and said, 'Surely the LORD is in this place, and I did not know it.'" This is the aftermath of Jacob's dream experience about the ladder. He was saying, "I thought God wasn't here, but I had an encounter with God and that changed the way that I was thinking." Again we see something in Jacob we don't see in Esau. We see something in him that we don't see in his brother. This is likely the reason why God loved Jacob and hated Esau (Malachi 1:2-3). God hates that stubbornness in all of us.

Then notice Jacob changes the name of the place based on his experience. "He called the name of that place Bethel" (Gen. 28:19), which means "house of God".

In Genesis 31:7, Jacob had built his family and flocks. He was about to leave Laban and he said to his wives, "You know that I have served your father with all my strength, yet your father has cheated me and changed my wages ten times. But God did not permit him to harm me" (Gen. 31:6-7). The crucial phrase in Jacob's statement is "But God." Jacob has totally changed the way that he sees how a person gets ahead, prospers, and gets blessed. Previously we saw Jacob conniving against his father and even deceiving his brother to get him to sell his birthright. But Jacob was changing. Notice who got the credit: "Thus God had taken away the livestock of your father and given them to me." (Gen. 31:9).

Jacob got ahead. He attributed it to God. He changed the way he saw prosperity. Later, in Genesis 31:42, Jacob argued with Laban about who should get what at their parting of ways after so many years. "If the God of my father, the God of Abraham and the Fear of Isaac, had not been on my side, surely now you would have sent me away empty-handed. God saw my affliction and the labor of my hands and rebuked you last night."

Notice in Genesis 32:10 where he said to God, "I am not worthy of the least of all the deeds of steadfast love and all the faithfulness that You have shown to your servant" Previously, his attitude had been, "Not only am I worthy, but God won't give me what I deserve. So I'm going to get it for myself!" Now he is saying, instead, "I'm overpaid. I'm blessed. I have more than I deserve." Jacob attributes what he actually does have to the grace and the steadfast love of God. He is thinking differently.

Then, in Genesis 32:11, he said, "Please deliver me from the hand of my brother, from the hand of Esau, for I fear him." What did Jacob used to do when he was afraid? He would run. He would hide. He would cheat. He would steal. Now he prayed about his specific stronghold. He's changed his view of how things like that get dealt with.

I could give a lot more examples, but I'm including these in the hope that it would encourage you that, though this man has not arrived and though this man is not everything that God is going to make him, change was really going on.

> **Take a little survey of your life similar to what we just did with Jacob's. Over the last couple of decades, what traits have remained constant and what ones have been changed over time? What shifts in your thinking or behavior give you encouragement that God is working on you with His own timetable?**

I love this saying: *I'm not what I could be. I'm not what I should be—but I'm not what I was.* That's Jacob. That can be you and me.

> **End today's homework thanking God specifically for changes you've noticed in other members in your study group. Express your gratitude for the way God is helping all of you think differently.**

DAY 2
THAT GOOD THING CALLED REPENTANCE

The most frequently used word in the Old and New Testaments for this matter of changing your thinking, thinking differently, and changing your mind is the Greek word *metanoia*. It's the word for repentance.

In a moment I'd like you to read again the most concentrated teaching in all of God's Word on the subject of repentance. I have become convinced that repentance is not a place we visit; repentance is where we live.

James 3:2 reminds us, "We all stumble in many ways." If this is true—and it is true because God's Word says it's true—then repentance isn't a place you go and then you kind of get over it.

In 2 Corinthians 7:8-11 Paul says:

> *For even if I made you grieve with my letter, I do not regret it—though I did regret it, for I see that that letter grieved you, though only for a while. As it is, I rejoice, not because you were grieved, but because you were grieved into repenting. For you felt a godly grief, so that you suffered no loss through us. For godly grief produces a repentance that leads to salvation without regret, whereas worldly grief produces death. For see what earnestness this godly grief has produced in you, but also what eagerness to clear yourselves, what indignation, what fear, what longing, what zeal, what punishment! At every point you have proved yourselves innocent in the matter.*

That's what repentance does—it brings cleansing. That's why we can say repentance is a good thing.

Repentance is such a good thing. It is the message in the mouth of every Old Testament prophet. It doesn't matter whether it's Isaiah, Jeremiah, Ezekiel, or

Hosea. They all called on God's people to repent. It's still everything that really needs to be said.

It's not a different message in the New Testament. When John the Baptist showed up, what's was message? "Repent...Prepare the way of the Lord" (Matt. 3:2-3). John insisted everyone should repent. We read the same thing from the apostles in Mark 6:12, "So they went out and proclaimed that people should repent."

After telling the parable of the one lost sheep, Jesus made the application obvious: "Just so, I tell you, there will be more joy in heaven over one sinner who repents than over ninety-nine righteous persons who need no repentance" (Luke 15:7). In other words, a greater party breaks out in heaven when a sinner repents than over a church filled with people who think that they don't have anything to repent about. God hates that. That's Esau. God's heart is that we would be tenderhearted, and easily submissive, and quickly responsive to the workings of His Spirit.

When we get to the early church in Acts 2 and the gospel is going worldwide, the message might be expected to change. No. The subject of the first sermon was repentance. "And Peter said to them, 'Repent and be baptized every one of you in the name of Jesus Christ for the forgiveness of your sins, and you will receive the gift of the Holy Spirit'" (Acts 2:38). The message of repentance just doesn't get old. Acts 3:19-20 says, "Repent therefore, and turn back, that your sins may be blotted out, that times of refreshing may come from the presence of the Lord."

I might point out as we survey the New Testament that repentance is a gift from God. The most dangerous thing that a follower of Jesus can say is, "I'll repent when I'm ready. I'm not finished with this sin yet. I'm not finished with this selfishness yet. I'll repent when I'm good and ready."

Do you have any idea how dangerous that kind of talk is? Only God can bring you to a place of repentance.

God gives you repentance. He does. You can harden your heart and stiffen your will, but according to the Book of Genesis, "Then the LORD said, 'My Spirit shall not abide in man forever'" (Gen. 6:3). You could come to the place where God's not even trying to bring you to a place of repentance anymore. This is as serious as serious gets. You can't just put off repenting indefinitely.

If you've never given you life to Jesus Christ, turn from your sin this moment and embrace Christ by faith for your forgiveness and receive the free gift of eternal life. But if you claim to have made that decision, Hebrews 10 says this:

> For if we go on sinning deliberately after receiving the knowledge of the truth, there no longer remains a sacrifice for sins, but a fearful expectation of judgment, and a fury of fire that will consume the adversaries. Anyone who has set aside the law of Moses dies without mercy on the evidence of two or three witnesses. How much worse punishment, do you think, will be deserved by the one who has trampled underfoot the Son of God, and has profaned the blood of the covenant by which he was sanctified, and has outraged the Spirit of grace?
> **HEBREWS 10: 26-29**

That is an extremely uncomfortable question. Judgment has to begin at the house of God. We are the people who are supposed to be prolific in our repentance, continual in our stirring up of tenderhearted self-analysis, and bringing our sin before the Lord.

Our Savior says, "Those whom I love, I reprove and discipline, so be zealous and repent" (Rev. 3:19). *Zealous* is the idea of putting your energy into it, putting your passion into getting a fresh, deeper, vibrant place with the Lord.

Be more sensitive to the Lord as the days go on. Listen better. Think higher. Love more. Give God easier access to every area of your life as your days grow fewer and fewer. As Psalm 90:12 tells us, "Teach us to number our days." We only have so many days. These are awesome days in which we can hear God's gracious invitation:

> Come now, let us reason together, says the Lord: though your sins are like scarlet, they shall be as white as snow; though they are red like crimson, they shall become like wool.
> **ISAIAH 1:18**

As you end today, ask yourself how deeply you believe and practice the concept of living in repentance. Ask God to make you receptive to the five marks of genuine repentance that we will begin to look at tomorrow.

DAY 3

FIVE MARKS OF GENUINE REPENTANCE

Yesterday we looked Luke 3:8 which tells us to "bear fruits in keeping with repentance." Because repentance is such a big subject, we could study it every week. We could devote an entire year and not be wasting our time.

Charles Spurgeon, the great English preacher from a century ago, was preaching on repentance week after week. A woman came up to him after one of his sermons and said, "All you ever talk about is repentance. When are you going to preach on something else?" He answered, "When you repent, madam!"

Let's begin looking at the five marks of genuine repentance found in 2 Corinthians 7:9-11. Paul didn't lay them out in any specific order; he wasn't trying to give a chronology. Paul wasn't trying to give us a thorough accounting for everything related to repentance; he was just trying to give a sense of it. I'm going to present them in a progression that makes sense to me.

Paul was feeling the weight of his tough love toward the church, knowing some had been hurt by his tone or words. He said, "For even if I made you grieve with my letter, I do not regret it—though I did regret it, for I see that that letter grieved you, though only for a while" (2 Corinthians 7:8). No one wants to do that. Paul continued, "As it is, I rejoice, not because you were grieved, but because you were grieved into repenting" (v. 9). If the outcome of a hard-to-teach, hard-to-hear message and series like this one is that we actually think differently because we repented and changed, it will be worth all of it. Likewise, Paul could see a bigger picture. "For you felt a godly grief, so that you suffered no loss through us" (v. 9). No loving parent likes to discipline their child, but discipline shows love. As Paul described the response of the Corinthians, he mentioned the five fruits of repentance we will now examine.

First, a fruit of repentance is **grief over sin**. Paul also calls this "godly grief" twice. "For you felt a godly grief, so that you suffered no loss through us. For godly grief produces a repentance that leads to salvation" (2 Corinthians 7:9-10).

By the way, repentance precedes confession. First John 1:9 says, "If we confess our sins, he is faithful and just to forgive us our sins and to cleanse us from all unrighteousness." But real confession is a lot more than saying, "Whoops! I sinned. It's sin, God. Now we agree, so I'm cleansed from all unrighteousness." Trust me, God has a lot more to say about your sin than simply agreeing "It's sin."

In fact, you can't say what God says about your sin confession until you see what God sees. Repentance is the process of allowing God to change your mind's eye so you don't see your sin the same way. The first example of the change is to have grief over sin. This is what Paul meant by "godly grief."

That word grief there, *lupeo*, is used twenty-six times in the New Testament and half of those usages are in 2 Corinthians. Half of the 2 Corinthians usages are in this passage. Here we have 25 percent of the entire New Testament teaching on the feelings that accompany repentance. The word is *grief*. It literally means soul anguish. It's what the disciples felt when Jesus announced His death and resurrection in Matthew 17:23, "'And they will kill him, and he will be raised on the third day.' And they were greatly distressed." It's what the rich young ruler felt when he realized he loved his riches more than the opportunity to follow Jesus: "When the young man heard this he went away sorrowful, for he had great possessions" (Matt.19:22). Grief is literally soul pain as opposed to worldly grief.

Do you see the contrast in Paul's words? There's a worldly grief: "For godly grief produces a repentance that leads to salvation without regret, whereas worldly grief produces death" (2 Cor. 7:10). What does worldly grief produces death mean? Well, that can't possibly mean physical death or there would be no distinction.

If Jesus doesn't return beforehand, we're all going to die physically anyway. So that wouldn't mean much to say that worldly grief produces what everyone's already going to experience. Paul's not talking about the first death; he's talking about the second death—the lake of fire. Paul is talking about hell. When Romans 6:23 says, "For the wages of sin is death," Paul isn't talking about physical death. He was warning the Corinthians and us that a lifetime of shallow, worldly repentance leads to hell.

That's a lifetime of saying, "Sorry, God. Whoops! I did it again. I always do it." That's not the way a saved person talks.

What has been an example of godly grief in your life?

If we don't love the truth more, and if we don't love each other more or don't see a growing pattern of Christ-likeness in our lives, we may be settling for worldly repentance. If what we say and think is: *I'm sorry I feel bad. I'm sorry I got caught. I'm sorry I looked bad. I'm sorry you don't like this, God*—that's worldly repentance. Men who repent worldly are not changed. They're not safe. Women who repent with worldly grief are not changed. They'll do it again. Worldly grief is not grieving over sin.

Second, a fruit of repentance is also **repulsion toward sin**. The phrase in 2 Corinthians 7:11 is "For see what earnestness." Earnestness means haste, hurry, or diligence. It says, "I'm done with this!" There is also indignation—feelings of strong displeasure which results in saying, "What used to rouse me now repulses me. What used to please me now it sickens me." That's what repentance generates in us.

But of course in all sin there's deception. Because Satan is an angel of light, he makes things glitter and glow, but repentance includes detecting the rationalizations that allowed me to see something as being attractive that actually, ultimately, now, and eternally is ugly.

When was the last time you were earnest about dealing with sin?

In closing, pray for your fellow study members, that they will experience this week some fruit worthy of repentance.

FIVE MARKS OF GENUINE REPENTANCE (CONTINUED)

We've already looked at the ways godly grief and revulsion toward sin are integral to genuine repentance. A third fruit of repentance is **restitution toward others**. In 2 Corinthians 7:11, Paul said, "What punishment!" The New American Standard Bible translates *punishment* as "avenging of wrong;" New King James says, "What vindication!" Paul goes on, "What eagerness to clear yourselves ... At every point you have proved yourselves innocent in the matter" (v. 11). When repentance happens, immediately we are concerned about making things right whereever they can be made right.

Just like the prodigal in the pigpen, when he came to his senses (Luke 15:17), he didn't stay there another moment. He got up, went home, and made it right with his family. When repentance is sincere we want to seek restitution with the people our sin has injured, as soon as we can.

We say, "I'm not going to bed until I have made that phone call." "I'm going over to their house and I'll wait until they talk to me." "I'm going to do everything I can. And I'm going to keep trying." Because that's what repentance really does. You're not right with God until you've done everything you can to make it right with the people your sin injured.

Now, we don't burden people with our confession. You don't go to your wife and say, "Let me just tell you all that I've been doing." The confession flows out from the circle of knowing. You don't burden someone with harmful details. But if they ask you, you can't lie. Even if they do ask you and you tell the truth, you don't give all the details. Love covers. You don't make it worse, but you can't lie about it. As far as everybody who knows about your slanderous mouth, and as far as everybody who knows about your passive, indifferent selfishness, or whatever you're convicted about, you could just say to them, "I've been wrong in the way I've been acting. Please forgive me." We take action when we're genuinely repentant.

Fourth, a fruit of repentance is **revival toward God**. That's what is meant by Paul's phrase, "What fear, what longing, what zeal" (v.11), all emotions directed toward and inspired by God. One of the fruits of repentance is that you just have a fired up relationship with God again: mercy is showered upon you; grace is received; forgiveness is experienced; and new disciplines are established. There is such joy in that reawakened interaction with the Lord who has been right there all along.

And fifth, a final fruit of repentance involves **a new willingness to move forward without looking back**. As Paul put it, "You suffered no loss through us" (v. 9). There is real sorrow yet without regret. Real repentance isn't looking back; it's looking forward to the years that remain. It's saying, "I'm going to capitalize on the time that I have. And I'm going to be the person that God has called me to be."

Alright. It's time to repent. It's time to stop thinking about repenting and understanding repentance better and getting to some actual repentance before your Heavenly Father. You could get on your knees right where you are. If you want to repent, a good place to start would be to get as low as you can as fast as you can. Let God confront you, and repent.

I pray that God has spoken through this messenger directly into your heart about what really matters to Him in your life. I trust that you've had some experiences along the way in this series in which you felt a little like David felt after Nathan told him a story that had him all up in arms about the injustice of someone who had taken what didn't belong to him and wanting to bring down heavy justice on that scoundrel, only to have God's servant and friend pull the rug right out from under him: "Nathan said to David, 'You are the man!'" (2 Sam.12:7).

It was as if Nathan had said, "Hey, David! What do you think of the guy who do this despicable act?" To which David had replied, "That's awful. Let's give him a dose of retribution!" Then, Nathan nailed him with, "David, that story is your life. You're the man who did that."

Even though David had rationalized for a year and had committed betrayal and murder, he was cut to the heart and changed forever. The God who took in all of David's life in a moment, that eternal God who had said when David was a young boy chasing sheep, "The Lord has sought out a man after his own heart" (1 Sam. 13:14). That guy, God was willing to confront and bring to repentance.

What God loved in Jacob was not that he was perfect, but that he was changing. Jacob let God confront him, again and again, and Jacob changed his mind.

Just quiet your heart before the Lord. If you're kneeling in prayer, please don't wallow in generalities. Let the Spirit of God prick your heart about something specific. Confess that and forsake it: "You are right, God. I am wrong. What I have been doing, what I've done is sin. I have no excuse. I am grieved by my stubbornness. I see, maybe even for the first time, the damage that my stubbornness is doing. I will make it right with others."

How hard it is when we feel that those we have sinned against have also sinned against us? How very difficult it is to go to a person and simply rehearse your own sin and leave with God anything you see imperfectly that you think he or she may have done?

We have Jesus Christ. We have His Holy Spirit. We have the fellowship of others in this study—and our church. We can go and humble ourselves before one another. We want God to deal graciously with us. May God help us to deal graciously with others. May He graciously show us our own sin.

> **Bring your fellow study members before the Lord and ask Him to pour out on all of you a spirit of repentance that creates an atmosphere where He can do His best work.**

> **Take whatever time is necessary to sit quietly before the Lord, asking Him to help you see where repentance needs to take place in your life today. Keep the list of the fruit of repentance close by and you allow God to speak to you.**

DAY 5
REPENTANCE BREAKS STRONGHOLDS

The prodigal son is the poster boy for repentance in the Bible. Like I told you last week, we're going to stop talking about strongholds and actually think differently—now!

I've been encouraging you to let God confront you and then I asked the question I hoped you were asking: "And what's my part in that?"

We're on it now. I hope God got you to it this week on your own. But now we're playing catch-up if you haven't engaged. When God confronts us, the right response on our part is to repent.

Do you remember the prodigal son? It's one of those parables of Jesus that sooner or later fits every one of our lives. That guy acted like a pig, unable to see beyond his own snout. He came to his father and said, "Give me my inheritance. Give it to me now. Break up the family's assets. I want what I want and I want it now."

He was a disgusting person. Who would do that to their father? If you said to your dad, "I want my inheritance now," what are you saying? You're saying, "I wish you were dead. Let's pretend you are and just give me what I get when you're dead. I'll take it in cash."

That is awful. He was thinking like a pig, and then he went and lived like a pig with all of that filthy lifestyle that he was in. The Bible says that he "squandered his property in reckless living" (Luke 15:13). Again, that's the delicacy of how the Scripture presents things, and I don't want to exceed that.

He lived like a pig until reality caught up with him and he ended up moving in with the pigs. He was at a pig farm because he didn't have any money. When he had money, he bought his friends. When he was out of money, he was suddenly out of friends. He did what lazy pigs do. When he didn't have any more choices he got a job. He started working the only job he could find, in the pigsty. But he was so desperate because he was paid so poorly that he started looking at what the pigs were eating.

Then repentance broke into his life. "But when he came to himself" (Luke 15:17), pictures that moment when God graciously turned on the light and he saw himself as if standing in front of a mirror. That was it—the moment when he started to think differently. He had thought he was big time, but he didn't think that anymore. He thought he was better than his family, but he didn't think that anymore. He thought he knew better than God, but he didn't think that anymore.

If you have someone today who's living that prodigal life—maybe it's you, maybe it's someone you love—pray for them to come to his or her senses.

Notice one of the instruments God used to get the prodigal's attention: "And no one gave him anything" (Luke 15:16). How often do we keep people from going to ruins or from hitting rock bottom? We think we're helping them, but we're hurting them. They need to come to the end of themselves and we need to come to the end ourselves. I've needed to come to the end of myself. I hope you've experienced that many times in your life and trusted God as a result.

After the prodigal came to his senses and headed for home, then he said as he was walking and thinking to himself: "What's it going to be like when I get there? What's Dad going to say to me?"

So he started working on his speech. This is remarkable: "I will arise and go to my father, and I will say to him, 'Father, I have sinned against heaven and before you. I am no longer worthy to be called your son'" (v. 18-19).

He had to wonder if his dad would say, "WELL! Haven't you changed your tune, Mr. I-Wish-You-Were-Dead! Where's the money we gave you?" Nothing could have been further from the truth.

But just to understand repentance, that boy was showing all the marks of repentance. There was grief, humility, action, and no expectation that things would ever be the same. He was just wanting to make things as right as he could. His speech said it all: "I thought I was too big time for this family. I thought I was better. I even thought I didn't need God. Was I ever wrong!"

Just like Jacob, who thought he was better than everyone until discovering the truth, finally confessed: "I'm not even worthy of what You have given me, God. I'm surprised You let me still be on this earth."

When we're in Jacob's sandals we find ourselves praying to God and saying, "I'm surprised You even give me a chance to work through this study and hear a pastor pour out his heart about repentance, God. Why are You still chasing me, God? Why are You still trying to bring me to a good place? How could You love me that much? I know what I've done; You know what I've done. How can I still be here sensing Your grace toward me?"

But that's God. And that's why He gets worshiped and obeyed. That's why we come back to the Father every time we come to our senses. Just like the prodigal, we say, "I will arise and go to my father, and I will say to him" (Luke 15:18). That's the last part of repentance. It's in the mind: He came to his senses. It's in the emotions: "I am not worthy." It's in the will. Actually saying and then doing what we said we would do. When repentance is happening in your heart, you'll want to get a pen and a piece of paper fast because you'll be writing down all of your ideas about how you're going to be different.

If you are trapped in a cycle of sin/confess, sin/confess, sin/confess, it's because you haven't repented.

A.W. Tozer said, "Let us beware of vain and overhasty repentance, and particularly let us beware of no repentance at all" (*Man the Dwelling Place of God*, 1966). Hell will be filled with people who prayed a prayer but never really repented of their sin. True repentance is followed by faith. There has to be a turning from something before there is a believing in something; some people try to believe but they've never turned.

What do you think Tozer meant by "vain and overhasty repentance"? Have your efforts to approach God ever been marked by those dangers? How? What keeps repentance genuine for you?

I say this a thousand times a year: "If you would turn from your sin and embrace Jesus Christ by faith..." I always say it that way. You have to turn—that's the repentance. And you have to believe—that's the gospel. And that's not just the first step with Jesus, that's every single step for the rest of your life: turning from sin and believing in Christ.

It helps to get specific about the sins we need to turn from. Note the chart below. It includes three major sin categories and three strongholds that function under them. This is, again, just picking some specific strongholds to be repenting about all the time.

LET'S GET SPECIFIC ABOUT SIN

PRIDE	PLEASURE	PRIORITIES
Position	Sex	Self
Prestige	Substance	Others
Power	Stuff	God

- **Pride** in my position, in what I've achieved, and in my influence and power, all the features of a stronghold. How do you handle that?

- **Pleasure**, and the variety of ways and means that promise to make us feel good. It's a tempting stronghold because it promises satisfaction but can't ultimately deliver.

- **Priorities** which push me to define what's first in my life. If I'm not deliberately keeping God as first priority, strongholds will rise "against the knowledge of God" (2 Corinthians 10:5).

As you conclude today's homework, consider those three major areas of life. The struggle against strongholds is a running battle for life, not a single encounter in which victory is forever. We're going to discover next that repentance is an important crisis God uses to kick-start a process that will go on for a long time.

If there are significant strongholds raising their banners in your life right now, it's not too late to have the crisis of repentance that will get you moving in the right direction like never before.

> **As this week ends, lift up each of the members of your study group in prayer, continually asking God to do His good work in them, bringing repentance and causing them to think differently.**

WEEK 9

WHEN YOU FAIL TO THINK DIFFERENTLY

Welcome to this next-to-last, ninth session of Think Differently. *We trust these last two sessions will be of great encouragement as you continue your walk with God.*

Begin the session with prayer, asking God to help each of you absorb and remember all the lessons that have been presented in the sessions. Thank God again for including flawed characters like Jacob in His Word so that we would be able to see there is hope for flawed people like us. Take a few minutes to invite the group to reflect together on the experiences with repentance in the past week.

Use the following questions to expand the discussion in preparation for the DVD teaching.

It isn't easy to live a life of repentance. When have you been given a glimpse of what that looks like?

In what ways does ready repentance help us to think differently?

By this point most of us are convinced that our thinking influences everything we do. This week's teaching will give us tools to deal with the inevitable experiences of falling short.

How would you explain the statement: "Life is a process"?

Continue to hide God's Word in your heart with the theme passage for this series. Read together the following verses:

> *For though we walk in the flesh, we are not waging war according to the flesh. For the weapons of our warfare are not of the flesh but have divine power to destroy strongholds. We destroy arguments and every lofty opinion raised against the knowledge of God, and take every thought captive to obey Christ, being ready to punish every disobedience, when your obedience is complete.*
> **2 CORINTHIANS 10:3-6**

WATCH

COMPLETE THE VIEWER GUIDE BELOW AS YOU WATCH DVD SESSION 9.

Broken strongholds will battle to be _____.

When you fail in the _____ of thinking differently, you must return to the _____ of stronghold repentance.

When you fall back, do these four things:

1. _____ stronghold supports from your life.

Three Crucial Questions:

    a)   Where did I go _____?

    b)   What _____ me up?

    c)   What needs to be _____?

2. _____ your view of God with reality.

Six Faulty Views of God:

    a)   God is a _____.

    b)   God is a _____ _____.

    c)   God is a _____ boss.

    d)   God is an _____ father

    e)   God is a _____ grandpa.

    f)   God is a _____.

3. _____ reminders to think differently.

4. _____ your identity and calling in God.

DISCUSS THE DVD SEGMENT WITH YOUR GROUP,USING THE QUESTIONS BELOW.

Would you say that you are more encouraged or discouraged by the news that there's failure ahead for all of us in the process of thinking differently? Why is that your response?

How have you seen demolished strongholds battle to be rebuilt?

Which of the three "removal questions" did you find most helpful, and why? 1) Where did I go wrong?; 2) What tripped me up?; 3) What needs to be removed?

What are the differences between *crisis* and *process* as James is using the terms?

Without the crisis/process strategy, what happens when we fail?

How have you found your view of God affecting the way you respond to life?

James had a few suggestions, but what have you found useful as a "raised reminder" to think differently or to live in repentance?

Application: What is one personal insight from this session you know you will use this week? Take a few minutes with the group to pray with each other asking for God's help in living in repentance and pursuing the process of thinking differently.

This week's Scripture memory:

> *I appeal to you therefore, brothers, by the mercies of God, to present your bodies as a living sacrifice, holy and acceptable to God, which is your spiritual worship. Do not be conformed to this world, but be transformed by the renewal of your mind, that by testing you may discern what is the will of God, what is good and acceptable and perfect.*
> **ROMANS 12:1-2**

Assignment: Complete the daily lessons for this next week in preparation for the final group experience. At least once each day this week, ask yourself: "Am I living right now in crisis mode or in process mode?" Take steps depending on the answer and trust that God is working in your life. Pray daily for each of your group by name, asking God to help them think differently this week.

WHEN YOU FAIL TO THINK DIFFERENTLY, DO THIS

We have discovered during these weeks that in order to think differently we have to see our strongholds, those fortified places and stubborn patterns of thinking that are resistant to God's Word and God's will. Then we let God confront us and we repent.

That's the crisis of thinking differently, but it's followed very quickly with the process of thinking differently which brings with it the realization that this is a tough thing. When you've been thinking a certain way—not for weeks or for months but for years and decades—you can know it's wrong, you can agree with God that it's wrong, you can seek and receive His forgiveness for it through repentance, but you can fall right back into it.

We will see this in Jacob's life: Broken strongholds will battle to be rebuilt.

We still have to choose to think differently. Day by day, we have to "take every thought captive to the obey Christ" (2 Cor. 10:5).

Now in Genesis 33 to 35, after all that happened by the River Jabbok, Jacob reverted to old patterns. The default settings and strongholds in his life were still capable of making his life complicated. Incredibly, even though it says in Genesis 33:4, "But Esau ran to meet him and embraced him and fell on his neck and kissed him, and they wept," it was the very picture of a successful reunion, but Jacob was still controlled by fear. He still put off his brother. He lied.

God had confronted Jacob and Jacob had repented of his strongholds. He had essentially said, "I'm not excusing it anymore. I'm not defending it anymore. I know it's wrong." But it is still really tough to think differently moment by moment. It is more than likely that all of us are going to fall back when we try to change.

Simply letting God confront you and repenting to Him doesn't mean it's over yet.

That's the crisis, but now comes the process.

In fact what we're discovering this week is that when you fail in the process of thinking differently, which will be frequently, perhaps several times a day, you must return to the crisis of stronghold repentance.

DAY 1
REMOVE STRONGHOLD SUPPORTS FROM YOUR LIFE

When you fail in the process of thinking differently, you must return to the crisis of stronghold repentance.

I can't say it any more clearly than that. Where the trouble really comes—it's not how often you fall at first, it's how long you stay down, how long you justify it. Let's say you've had a bitter heart toward someone, and God has confronted you. You've repented of your bitterness and unforgiveness, and you've chosen to forgive the person. Then, a day later, you're mad again, and you're thinking the way you were before. Don't accept those old arguments. Don't accept those lofty opinions that are exalting themselves against the knowledge of God.

Take every thought captive to obey Christ and say: "I'm not that person anymore. I'm not going to think that way anymore. I'm not going to defend this—I'm going to repent again. And I'm going to pray, 'God, we made a promise to one another. And You're going to help me. And I'm not going to excuse this anymore.'"

What do we do when we fall back? Once again we turn to the life we've been tracking the last few weeks. When we last spent time with Jacob, he had a life-altering encounter with God. We watched him limp away, disheveled from wrestling all night, with a new and hopeful name.

In what ways have you seen demonlished strongholds and broken patterns return with a vengeance that surprised you?

What is your answer for spiritual failure?

In Genesis 33, Jacob fell back. In the light of the new day, Esau and his four hundred men still looked scary to Jacob, and he couldn't resist the stronghold of managing the situation to protect himself. He had met God face to face, but he was still capable of fear. Esau turned out to be the opposite of Jacob's expectations. Almost three decades had passed, and Esau has gotten on with his life. Jacob was weighed down by his past choices. Things were right with God, but they were not right with his brother, although Esau didn't care. Jacob didn't know what to do with the misplaced dread he had developed over the coming reunion. His solution was to avoid and distance himself from a genuinely welcoming brother.

We skipped over Genesis 34, even though it shows Jacob's stronghold of passivity, but the main lesson in that chapter has to do with the way Jacob's sons had picked up family sins and were acting out generational patterns.

In Genesis 35, God confronted Jacob again. Jacob had bought land in Shechem and settled there, only to have all kinds of problems. He was not where God wanted him. "God said to Jacob, 'Arise, go up to Bethel and dwell there. Make an altar to the God who appeared to you when you fled from your brother Esau" (v. 1). It was time for déjà vu for Jacob. God reminded him of everything that occurred at the Jabbok River. The Lord was creating a crisis for Jacob by calling him back to the place of his repentance and bringing up the stronghold of fear that had been the subject of his repentance.

It's important for us to see with Jacob that when we drift or fall back from His way into former strongholds, we will have to repent and say, "This is wrong, Lord. It was wrong before and it's wrong again. And I do repent. And I'm not excusing it anymore. I'm not thinking the same way about it. I don't feel the same way about it. I'm forming a plan of action to do differently."

What we see in Jacob's response in Genesis 35:1-2, 4 is the first steps we can take when we realize we have failed to think and to act differently. We're moving in the right direction when we remove stronghold supports from our lives.

Jacob knew he needed to obey God's instruction, but he realized that there were some immediate steps to take: "So Jacob said to his household and to all who were with him, 'Put away the foreign gods that are among you and purify yourselves and change your garments'" (vv. 1-2). Though we know he had been painfully passive much of the time, when he stepped up and led his family, they actually followed. "So they gave to Jacob all the foreign gods that they had, and the rings that were in their ears. Jacob hid them under the terebinth tree that was near Shechem" (v. 4).

What Jacob did here tells us he asked the three questions we will examine tomorrow: 1) Where did I go wrong? 2) What tripped me up? 3) What needs to be removed? With God's help, our answers to these questions will lead us to remove the supporting components from certain strongholds in our lives, diminishing the possibility that they will be back soon or with such control over us.

God will use multiple crises and a long process in your life to bring about all He has planned. As you close today's homework, thank God for both crises and process. Thank Him in particular for the crisis that first brought you salvation by faith in Christ. Thank Him for the process and progress in sanctification He has been working out in your life. Thank Him for the gift of repentance and His persisted willing to wade into your life and wrestle with you until you get the point.

Pray again for your fellow study members.

THREE KEY CRISIS QUESTIONS

So if you fall back, and when you fail, here are three questions that need to be answered:

1) WHERE DID I GO WRONG?

Where did Jacob fall into being under the influence of his strongholds again? Jacob was going along in the post-Laban weeks when the anticipation of meeting Esau brought on a crisis with his stronghold of fear. God met him, and he repented of it, realizing that this is not what he wanted.

He made his way back, limping, but he was on the road again. But here comes his brother and Jacob gets fearful. Then comes this situation with this daughter and Jacob gets all passive. He's in the ditch and just beginning to realize it.

When you find yourself back in the stronghold ditch, you have to figure out, "Where did I go off the road?" You have to make your way back. Now repentance includes identifying the contributing factors.

God comes to Jacob again and confronts him. Jacob has to do a little bit of an analysis here.

I talked to a man this week who was repenting. I just asked him, "But why did you do this?" After he kind of explained to me, I said, "When did this start? This isn't who I knew you to be." He told me. He knew right where he went wrong. He pin-pointed it. He could describe the sequence that God had interrupted and brought him to his knees. Honestly, I don't judge him because I really relate to his experience. He has a stronghold and is dealing with it, and God is helping him.

I've often repeated the stat that life is 10 percent what happens to you and 90 percent how you respond. Something may have happened to you like happens to many other people, but because you responded a certain way, your strongholds got a new lease on life. Where did that happen? Repent. Make your way back. It may have been decades ago or last week. That was then; what are you going to do now? And what will you do if it happens again?

2) WHAT TRIPPED ME UP?

In Jacob's instance, apparently it was these foreign gods. When Jacob set up his tent on his lot in Shechem, Genesis 33:20 says, "There he erected an altar and called it El-Elohe-Israel," which means "God, the God of Israel." This was his personal testimony to his neighbors that he would be making offerings to his God, the One with whom he had wrestled. But a chapter later, it's clear his family hasn't been in sync with Jacob. They had some particular idols of some kind, some false gods. I can't say it any clearer than that. They had false gods that they were bowing down to.

> **If you're battling your stronghold, what is it that you're turning to instead of God?**

Jacob struggled to think differently. But he wanted victory, so he is did a fierce moral and physical inventory of his heart and of his house.

You should be thinking right now, *What strongholds are in my home that I lean on instead of God?* Jacob's immediate trip wire was false gods; what's yours?

I don't care if it's a chocolate cake. If you're turning to something other than to God, that's a problem. Once it's identified, repentance calls for some radical action.

3) WHAT NEEDS REMOVAL?

Genesis 35:2 describes the instructions given for idol abatement: "So Jacob said to his household and to all who were with him, 'Put away the foreign gods that are among you.'" Jacob was announcing, "We're not doing that anymore. That's been part of our problem." But he's not finished: "And purify yourselves and change your garments."

Verse four tells us they gave them all to him—all of the idols and everything, like ear rings that may have had religious purposes. Perhaps Rachel pulled out her father's household idols and finally got rid of them.

Lots of things can represent our willingness to trust things other than God:

Maybe it's something you wear.
Maybe it's a style you have that is not modest.
Maybe it's just some way that you've been thinking.

One place to start is to ask yourself, do I have anything or any relationship that I would not willingly and immediately hand over to God if He asked?

We really don't know exactly what Jacob ended up with when the household piled up their idols, but what he did next was curious. Genesis 35:4 goes on to say, "Jacob hid them under the terebinth tree that was near Shechem."

Really, Jacob? Did you hide them? You're not supposed to hide them; you're supposed to smash them. That's what you do with idols. You don't mess around with it. You don't put your idols temporarily out of reach somewhere where they might be retrieved later. Do you want to think differently or not?

I don't believe unaccountable time and activities are freedom; I believe those are the pathway to bondage. Thankfully I'm not in bondage, and you don't have to be either.

Our theme passage in 2 Corinthians 10:3-6 includes a picture of intellectual idols. These are removed when we "destroy arguments and every lofty opinion" so our thinking and worldview always begin with God and His Word. Strongholds are not easily defeated or demolished. They call for radical action.

The underlying principle is this: Whatever feeds your stronghold must be put out of] reach. Otherwise, you will go back to it in a moment of weakness. Whatever protects and reinforces your stronghold must be put out of your reach or you won't think differently.

I may not know you personally, but "I am confident of better things concerning you" (Heb. 6:9, NKJV).

And we are going to think differently.

If you know someone who's in the ditch right now, pray for them. What else might you do to encourage them?

If they are part of this study, you can remind them of these principles. Otherwise, simply let them know you're praying and you're available.

Make sure you are being thorough in asking the three questions when you realize you need to repent in an area and get back on track.

RECONCILE YOUR VIEW OF GOD WITH REALITY

After removing the stronghold supports from your life, as we have been doing the last two days, here's the second strategic move we can pick up from Jacob. It's in Genesis 35:3, 5. You're carting out all the bad stuff and in its place you reconcile your view of God with reality.

At the end of the day, the battle is over of what you believe about God. We can trace a sad track record for humanity beginning with the Garden of Eden where Satan attacked Eve's view of God. Read Genesis 3 to see the subtle challenging of Eve's understanding of God. Satan said, "Has God really said...? Is that what He said? I don't think He said that! If He did say that, He didn't say it for a good reason. I think He's tricking you. You can't trust God." By the time he was done, her thinking was so twisted that she did the very thing God had specifically said not to do.

Satan doesn't have a lot of plays; he just packages things up in different ways. He is throwing the same stuff in front of you that he was throwing all of those years ago. He wants to mess up the way you think about God because a wrong view of God leads to wrong thinking, which leads to wrong behavior. You can't change your behavior if you can't change your thinking. And you can't change your thinking if you don't change your thinking about God.

If someone asked you what God is like, how would you begin your answer?

What aspects of God's character mean the most to you?

Watch that happen with Jacob right here in the text. Genesis 35:3 says, "Then let us arise and go up to Bethel, so that I may make there an altar to the God who answers me in the day of my distress and has been with me wherever I have gone."

You can't keep from struggling in the process to think differently, but you can repent and go right back to it and never just go on excusing it.

Look at his phrases in Genesis 35:3. "God who answers me" is Jacob's theology. God answers, therefore He is good. Even though a lot of the problems had been Jacob's fault, God was good to him. Jacob understands, "God is always with me; therefore, He is faithful."

Genesis 35:5 gives us a picture of the effects that surround someone moving under the protection of the good and faithful God: "And as they journeyed, a terror from God fell upon the cities that were around them." God didn't want Jacob to get into trouble so He caused fear to infect everyone so that Jacob could travel in peace. Jacob could conclude, "God protects me; He is gracious."

Contrast Jacob's experience with the distorted thinking about God listed below. The god of this world has no power against the strongholds in our lives. It's time to see these distortions and correct them.

SIX FAULTY VIEWS OF GOD

You might have some of these wrong views of God that are part of the stronghold.

- **Faulty View #1.** God is not wise. He is just a killjoy with all the rules in the Bible designed to keep me from being happy.

That is a lie. God's rules are not forbidding things that would make you happy; they're protecting you from things that would lead to misery. Deuteronomy 30:19 says, "I have set before you life and death, blessing and curse. Therefore choose life." There is a God that loves you. He is not a discourager. That's just bad theology.

- **Faulty View #2.** God is a prison warden, always watching us. God wants to take away our freedom.

Again, that's just bad theology. There is so much freedom in following Christ: "And you will know the truth, and the truth will set you free" (John 8:32). Often I have wandered from the path that God lays out for me and felt the sting of what He forbids. Never have I been disappointed when I followed in what He commends for my joy.

- **Faulty View #3.** God isn't fair, just like a cranky boss. He's demanding, critical, and never satisfied.

 God's not like that—at all. Zephaniah 3:17 says, "He will rejoice over you with gladness; He will quiet you by his love; He will exult over you with loud singing." It is so awesome to think that God looks at all of us fallen like we are, but in Christ He is like swinging a tambourine and rejoicing over us. He sees us at our worst, but He stands outside of time, and He knows how He's going to perfect and complete you until the day of Jesus Christ. He is not riding the roller coaster of our ups and downs. He is rejoicing over us with singing.

- Faulty View #4. God is an absent Father, never around when you need Him.

I'm sorry if your father was missing in action, but God is not your dad. Thank God that He's not your dad. The best of fathers see their own failures. I certainly am aware of my deficiencies. But God is not an absent Father. And He is very attentive to you. If that's an issue for you, you should memorize Romans 8:35, 38-39, "Who can separate us from the love of God? ... For I am sure that neither death nor life, nor angels nor rulers, nor things present nor things to come, nor powers, nor height nor depth, nor anything else in all creation, will be able to separate us from the love of God in Christ Jesus our Lord."

That's theology, man! That is what is actually true. Down with thinking lies! Up with thinking about what's true.

- **Faulty View #5.** God is a moody Grandpa who is unpredictable, capricious, fickle, and erratic. You never know what's going to set Him off. One day He's giving you candy and the next day He's yelling at you.

God is not like that. He is the same always. "For I the LORD do not change" (Mal. 3:6).

- **Faulty View #6.** God is a scorekeeper. You could be playing the game and then one thing goes wrong and then all of a sudden God is red-carding you.

God is not like that. He is not keeping a record of our wrongs. All of our sins—past, present, and future— are covered in Jesus. Isn't that incredible? God has never once diminished His love for you. Never. It has always been at maximum. Nothing you can do earns that love; nothing you can do changes that love. That is reality.

When someone tells you they don't believe in God, ask that person to describe for you the God they don't believe in. In all likelihood they will describe a god very much like the god of one of these distortions. When they are finished, you can say, "You're right, I don't believe in that god either."

If you're having a hard time getting to this view of God, think differently. "Be trans- formed by the renewal of your mind" (Rom. 12:2), by the Word of God. God has told us plenty and clearly about Himself. He has stepped into His own universe as Jesus Christ to give us the greatest experience of Himself. Step into the life that He has purchased for His children through the sacrifice of His own Son.

End your homework time today with a few minutes of simply telling God all the things that you appreciate about Him. You could also note them here.

RAISE REMINDERS TO THINK DIFFERENTLY

When you have failed to think differently and God has graciously gotten you back on the right track, take a page from the play book of many people in the Bible and raise reminders that will help you steer clear of dangerous areas and draw your attention back to God. Post signs on your life road that will encourage you to remember what God has done and who He is. Give yourself hints that provoke thinking differently. That's what Jacob did.

Notice in Genesis 35:6-7, "And Jacob came to Luz (that is, Bethel), which is in the land of Canaan, he and all the people who were with him, and there he built an altar and called the place El-bethel [El is God and bethel means house of God, so this is an emphatic God's house of God], because there God had revealed Himself to him." Jacob has already done this naming back in Genesis 28:19 when he first left home, "He called the name of that place Bethel." He was back at the same place where God met him. In his dream he had seen the ladder between earth and heaven and in the morning he set up a pillar and poured oil on top of it.

Now he was back doing the same thing, in the same place, with the same God. Jacob did it again. This was a review. This was a reminder. The point was that he had raised a reminder to think differently, and he introduced his family to his experience.

Here's what Jacob was doing. He was raising visible cues. We identify visible cues to change our thinking and to keep ourselves on track. You put things in your life that you can see, that you can recognize, that will help you remember that you can say, "I don't think like that anymore."

Take out the strongholds and destroy anything that was supporting them. Put things in your life that are visual cues of remembrance. Put a picture on your dashboard in your car—something that will make you think about thinking differently. You could post something by your refrigerator. You could place a framed copy of a significant Bible passage on your nightstand. I don't know if this is the right time of year, but you could plant a tree and use it as a living signpost to remind you of a life-changing encounter with God.

You see, that's what Jacob is did at Bethel—he put up some rocks; he poured some oil on it; he consecrated himself; he had a time of prayer; and he named the location for spiritual significance.

Maybe God has met with you in a powerful way in the worship area of your church. That place has become holy ground to you. Letting that space or place remind you of what God has done can be a healthy trigger to focus your thoughts on Him rather than letting your mind drift. It may be time to decide, *I'm just going to come and sit in this room, and I'm just going to talk to God about how I'm thinking differently, how I don't want to go back, and how I want this to last forever—to be a true change in my life.*

You could start with a card in your Bible, named Significant Sites: Places Where God Met Me. List them by location. Include dates if possible. Note Scriptures that were part of God's work in you. Let this become a testimony to your family of the way God has repeatedly intersected the journey of your life as He did Jacob's.

Remarkably, in Genesis 35:9, "God appeared to Jacob again." After God met with Jacob and Jacob responded with worship and recognition, God continued the interaction. James 4:8 urges us, "Draw near to God, and he will draw near to you."

Have you considered what this would involve in your own life? The actions you take because you want to think differently about everything and especially about God are not going to go unnoticed. When you make a move toward God, He will never back away. Drawing near starts with acknowledging God's presence in your circumstances and history. This is part of what Jesus meant in Matthew 6:33 when He instructed us to counter worry and anxiety in our lives by the choice to "seek first the kingdom of God and his righteousness." In contrast to everything the world is seeking (Matt. 6:32), we are to be on the lookout for God's activity and power in the world. If we seek, we'll find. And when we find places where God is working, let's make it a point to remember them. Those places become Bethel, the house of God—the kingdom of God.

I watched my own father struggle after the death of my mom, wrestling with God over grief and the need to let someone go who had been his beloved wife of more than half a century. Part of it came down to the finality of placing her gravestone.

It was both a strong symbol of memory but also an important act of release. Eventually, he had to take some action to communicate to himself the treasure of that extended time with my mother and highlight that it was now a memory rather than an ongoing reality. His grief was a hard season, but when the gravestone was placed, that season was marked ended. Dad was ready to ask, "What does God have for me now?"

This is why we raise reminders to think differently. Whether it's something that has to go or something you put in its place, let the changes that you make to the landscape of your life be shouting to you, "That's not you anymore." You're ready for what God has next.

If you're going to start a "Significant Sites" card, do it right now as you end this day's assignment.

Before closing in prayer take a mental survey of your history and the ways God has managed to show up at various moments along the way. Rejoice over His grace toward you.

Thank God again for the evidences of His work in the lives of each person who has been part of this study with you.

REVIEW YOUR IDENTITY AND CALLING IN THE LORD

Here's the step you can take that sets your feet firmly back on the road of following hard after God. You've had the crisis when God caused you to realize you have taken a detour into the ditch. You have repented. You're ready to resume the process God wants to use in shaping you. First, you cut the supply lines of the strongholds in your life. Then, you've updated and clarified you view of God to remove distortions. Once you have raised the sacred reminders that point to God's gracious intervention, it's time to review your identity and your calling in the Lord. Watch this happened for Jacob in Genesis 35:9-10, "God appeared to Jacob again, when he came from Paddan-aram, and blessed him. And God said to him, 'Your name is Jacob.'"

Pause for a moment and consider what God is saying. The name Jacob describes the bent character of Isaac and Rebekah's son, ruled by strongholds. We saw that character on display in Genesis 33 and 34. There was still a lot of work for God to do in the man who bore that name, and He began by giving Jacob a new name. Verse 10 says, "And God said to him, 'Your name is Jacob; no longer shall your name be called Jacob, but Israel shall be your name.'"

We look down at our Bible pages and think, *Didn't that just happen? Didn't we read that God said this about a page back?*

Yes it did, and yes, we did read that back in Genesis 32:28. Isn't God gracious to come back and remind us of what's true when our thinking slips back into what is not true? I hope that's been happening this week for you and even right now God can see you working on this homework. I hope He's reminding you of what's true and what isn't.

A big part of what God wants you to know in your deepest recesses is your own identity, the way He sees you. God was saying to His flawed servant Jacob, "Your name no longer shall be Jacob. Your name Jacob means liar. You're not a liar anymore. You're not a cheater anymore. You might still battle that temptation, but that's not who you are."

When God moves toward you, two things have to happen: 1) your view of God has to change, and 2) your view of yourself has to change. These changes are intended parts of the process every day, though we see it most clearly in the times of crisis when God has to interrupt a drift or fall to put us back on track. For your thinking to be good, your view of God has to change, and your view of yourself has to change.

Those two things should the continual focus of attention as you live each day: how you see God and how you see yourself.

As a brief exercise, take a piece of paper and write a paragraph under each of these headings. Emphasize the way God Himself has been involved in your perspectives:

1. How I saw God and how I saw myself in childhood.

2. How I saw God and how I saw myself five years ago.

3. How I see God and how I see myself right now.

4. Ways I realize my view of God and myself need to change.

Jacob fell back, and God's came right at him. God invited him for another appointment at Bethel. Jacob knew he couldn't show up dragging baggage filled with foreign gods and symbols of paganism. He saw how God had brought terror into the people who might have made his passage to Bethel a problem. And, he knew that arriving in Bethel should include the deliberate building of an altar to declare the place as actually God's house. Jacob began to know God and saw Him at work in his life. Just as significantly, Jacob realized that God really knew him.

When we know God better, we see ourselves more clearly—always a healthy experience. Despite our temptation to manage our image before God, the truth is that God knows us better than we know ourselves. God has an intended calling over our lives that He knows better than we do. Why wouldn't we want to accept what He says to us about us? He knows who we are, like He knew everything about Jacob, but He didn't hesitate to give Jacob a new name.

For decades maybe you have fought with God, argued with God, or lied to get your way. Then God took you down and laid you out. Like Jacob, you have to change your view of God and change your view of yourself.

You are not a liar anymore. You have a new name. Instead of wrestling with God, you're following Christ. It's time to think differently: to think differently about God and to think differently about yourself.

As you conclude this week's assignments, pray over the last session in the study. Ask God to be powerfully present as you meet and discuss the life-altering power of thinking differently.

With the end of the study in sight, consider having an intentional plan for encouraging the spiritual disciplines you have been practicing during the *Think Differently* study.

Pray for each of your group's members by name, asking God to highlight for them this week new ways they can see Him and clearer ways they can see themselves.

WEEK 10

HOW TO RENEW YOUR MIND

Welcome to the tenth and final session of this group discussion of Think Differently.

After a prayer time, use the following questions to expand the discussion while encouraging everyone to participate.

Tell us a favorite personal highlight from the last nine weeks of this study and its effects.

Describe one subject or situation that has changed because you are now thinking differently.

Sooner or later we need to consider how to make changes in our minds that will shape the way we think. This session will give us some long range and lifelong tools for renewing and maintaining a mind that can think differently.

To prepare for this session's teaching, read the following verses together as a group:

> *Now this I say and testify in the Lord, that you must no longer walk as the Gentiles do, in the futility of their minds. They are darkened in their understanding, alienated from the life of God because of the ignorance that is in them, due to their hardness of heart. They have become callous and have given themselves up to sensuality, greedy to practice every kind of impurity. But that is not the way you learned Christ!—assuming that you have heard about him and were taught in him, as the truth is in Jesus, to put off your old self, which belongs to your former manner of life and is corrupt through deceitful desires, and to be renewed in the spirit of your minds, and to put on the new self, created after the likeness of God in true righteousness and holiness.*
> **EPHESIANS 4:17-24**

WATCH

COMPLETE THE VIEWER GUIDE BELOW AS YOU WATCH DVD SESSION 10.

Think differently or live to _____ it.

_____ is when the verdict lands with finality: "I have no one to blame, but myself."

Real _____ is turning upward to _____ , outward toward _____ , and not inward to _____ .

Express faith that confessed _____ leads to _____ .

Faith is _____ in the Word of God, _____ upon it, no matter how I feel, because God promises a good _____ .

Jacob always bore the _____ of the strongholds he stubbornly maintained.

Thinking differently means _____ your mind. (Eph. 4:17-24; Rom. 12:1-2)

How to renew your mind:

1. _____ your mind.

2. _____ your mind.

Deepen your commitment to God's Word:

- _____
- _____
- _____

3. _____ your mind.

DISCUSS THE DVD SEGMENT WITH YOUR GROUP, USING THE QUESTIONS BELOW.

What lessons do you take away from the reality that Jacob never really changed?

Are some regrets unavoidable? How does someone avoid living a regret filled life?

Read Hebrews 11:21. What did James mean by his point about having faith that confesses weakness leads to blessing?

Proverbs 24:16 says, "For the righteous falls seven times and rises again, but the wicked stumble in times of calamity." What does this verse have to do with the importance of renewing our minds?

James offered three components to the ongoing process of renewing our mind: protect your mind, wash your mind, and set your mind. Explain each of these in your own words.

Which of these three actions represent what you know you need to be more diligent in doing? Why?

Thinking about the totality of Jacob's life, what are one or two things you don't want to ever have regrets about by the end of your life (even if today is it)?

Application: After ten teaching sessions we're still grappling with the truth that nothing is really different until we think differently. Each of us still has strongholds we haven't seen demolished and perhaps others we haven't even identified yet. Take a few minutes with the group to pray for each other. Ask for God's help in the ongoing process of letting God change us into people who really do think differently.

This week's Scripture memory:

> *If then you have been raised with Christ, seek the things that are above, where Christ is, seated at the right hand of God. Set your minds on things that are above, not on things that are on earth.* **COLOSSIANS 3:1-2**

Assignment: Complete the daily lessons for this next week. Continue daily day to pray for each of your group by name, asking God to help them think differently into the future.

HOW TO RENEW YOUR MIND

Thinking differently—if it were easy, everyone would be doing it. The fact is that it is not easy to think differently. The reason it's not easy is because of these things called strongholds—by way of a little review—a stubborn pattern of thinking that is resistant to God's Word and to God's will for us. That concept of strongholds comes from our theme verses:

> For the weapons of our warfare are not of the flesh but have divine power to destroy strongholds. We destroy arguments and every lofty opinion raised against the knowledge of God, and take every thought captive to obey Christ. **2 CORINTHIANS 10:4-5**

We have been learning that nothing is different until we think differently. To do that, we have learned to do something about our strongholds. Here are the three steps:

1. Step one was to discover the source of the strongholds. We looked at strongholds in our disposition, in our family dysfunction, and that came from our own decisions and desires.

2. In step two, we went to the crisis of changing our thinking. When you fail in the process of thinking differently, you have to return to the crisis of repenting and resume the process. You've probably been doing that as I have been, even multiple times a day.

3. This week we are on step three, which is living the moment by moment details of actually thinking differently. It's about renewing our minds.

In the final analysis of Jacob's life we must face this reality: Jacob did not change. In spite of all of the grace that was given to him, all of the time that was given to him, and all of the opportunities that were given to him, Jacob didn't change.

Jacob summarized his life with one word: evil. His life was regrettable. Regret names those dark shadows over your life: what should have been, what could have been, what would have been if you had let God work. Regret is when the verdict lands with finality: You have no one to blame, but yourself. When the blimp of reality lands on you, you recognize—like Jacob finally had to—regret. This is motivation to think differently, or you'll live to regret it. God wants to renew you mind.

DAY 1

THE BENEFIT OF CONFESSED WEAKNESS

Hebrews 11 lists the greatest faith people in the Bible all the way back. It includes Abel, Enoch, and Noah. Verse 8 is the beginning of the patriarchs with Abraham, but I want to start with Sarah, Abraham's wife. Hebrews 11:11 says, "By faith Sarah herself received power to conceive, even when she was past the age, since she considered him faithful who had promised." Sarah was too old to have kids, having never even had any kids. Then, at ninety, she gave birth to Isaac.

Underline the words "she considered" in your Bible.

The word *consider* there literally means to press down your mind upon. She took some time to think about it. She pondered all the options and responses and she arrived at a conclusion: "She considered Him faithful who had promised." After she waited, doubted, struggled, and even laughed over the outrageous idea of a pregnancy, Sarah came to a place of faith: "Well, it is God who is telling me this. And He has kept every promise He has ever made. So I'm going to go with it." She demonstrated herself to be a woman of faith.

Faith is believing in the Word of God, and acting upon it, no matter how I feel, because God promises a good result.

In Hebrews 11:17-19 we return to Abraham to see this same working of faith, "He [Abraham] considered that God was able even to raise him [Isaac] from the dead" (v. 19). That's the same as his wife Sarah. He took some time to think differently, basing his actions on his understanding of God even though obedience placed his son's life at risk.

There are a lot of people today who say, "God's asked me to do something very hard." Compared to what Abraham was asked to do (sacrifice his son), what we call "hard" usually means, "It's hard because I don't want to do it" or "It's hard because it's inconvenient." We're forgetting who we're talking about if we say, "God shouldn't be asking me to do hard stuff." It's actually exactly what God gets to do.

But God always has our good in mind when He asks us hard things. When Abraham went through the steps of putting his son Isaac on an altar Abraham learned that if Isaac could be sacrificed, he couldn't become an idol for Abraham. Isaac had to realize he was not more important to his father than God was. Even when God says, "Don't!", what He means is, "Don't hurt yourself!"

How did Abraham pull it off? Hebrews 11:19 indicates he was thinking, *It doesn't matter what I'm asked because this is the promised kid. God is in charge of his life. God will stop me at the end or He will raise him up afterwards.* The solution to an impossible problem keeps God in the picture. Abraham only had to focus on obedience; he left the ultimate results in God's hands.

That's the response of faith. But you don't get there in five seconds; Abraham had to think about that a lot and get his mind on it. The decades of waiting for Isaac's arrival must have filled his thinking as he walked with Isaac for days to the mountain where God affirmed his faithful obedience (Gen. 22).

Hebrews next mentions Isaac's faith and then brings up Jacob, the man whose painful story we have traveled these weeks. We don't get paragraphs or even great sentences about Jacob. Yet, he somehow, by God's grace, surprisingly makes the list here. Hebrews 11:21 simply says, "By faith Jacob, when dying, blessed each of the sons of Joseph, bowing in worship over the head of his staff."

What a funny thing to point out, right? It reads like a deathbed conversion. At the end of Jacob's life, he blessed his kids, and he worshiped God. Some translations say he did this while "leaning" on his staff. That is the last mention of Jacob in the Bible. At the very end, he was bowing and leaning.

This was the guy who was always wrestling with God to the extent that God touched his hip and gave him a limp. He carried a double name, Jacob/Israel, the "grabber" and the "wrestler with God." What we have here is a picture of Jacob, weak to the very end. Even though Jacob loved God, even though he prayed over his kids, even though Jacob worshiped to the last day, he didn't let God have His way in his life so Jacob was weak to the very end. Hebrews 11:21 shows us a painful, final summary: Jacob always bore the scars of the strongholds he stubbornly maintained.

As you come to the end this study, this picture of Jacob is one you should carry with you. Carry it because it reminds you (and me) of a reality that will also be true of us. We will reach the end of life unfinished. God will be working on us to the last moment. One of the best things we can say is, "Not perfectly, but increasingly I am seeing Christ formed in me as God helps me think differently." We will be mostly fighting or mostly submitting every step of the way. Here's the best news about that sad picture of Jacob: God still loved that scared, sinful, struggling-to-live-out-his-faith, old man. God remained patient. He kept showing up. He accepted Jacob's final worship.

You and I will experience throughout our entire lives some of the scarring resulting from our strongholds, like Jacob did, but our last picture doesn't have to be as sad as his was. God wants to take us further and accomplish more in our lives. As I've noted, it won't matter along the way how often we have fallen, but the difference will be seen in how long we stay down. God will be with you, as He was with Jacob, every step of the way.

When (not if) you fall, how will you get back up and keep moving?

Because I've been saying for weeks in this series, "Nothing is different until you think differently," let me say in the positive now as we move through this final week, "Everything is different when we think differently." This is where it begins and ends. We have to think differently about everything, and God needs to be a part of every-thing we think.

Don't miss the Bethel moments of your life when God shows up to let you know He loves you. Best not to wrestle with Him over that; accept His love.

If today was your last day, about what things would you have to admit God still has a lot of work to do in you to demolish strongholds? Talk to Him about those matters.

Pray again for your other study members as God continues to do His work in them even during this final week.

DAY 2

THINKING DIFFERENTLY- RENEWING YOUR MIND

It is unbelievable of how many references there are to the mind, to thinking, throughout the Bible, particularly in the New Testament. But even if there weren't all that many, Jesus' words would have to rivet our attention. When asked point-blank what was the most important thing expected of us as human beings, His answer was equally direct: "The most important is, 'Hear, O Israel: The Lord our God, the Lord is one. And you shall love the Lord your God with all your heart and with all your soul and with all your mind and with all your strength.' The second is this: 'You shall love your neighbor as yourself.' There is no other commandment greater than these" (Mark 12:29-31). Loving God with all our mind was part of the bottom line commandment from the Lord. There are plenty of guidelines from God's Word about what it's going to take to love the Lord as we should.

Ephesians 4:17 says, "Now this I say and testify in the Lord, that you must no longer walk as the Gentiles do in the futility of their minds." Just in case you didn't get the equality memo, if you don't have Jewish ancestry, you're in with the rest of us Gentiles. Paul is talking about a big problem: foolish thinking which leads to foolish living. If your mind is consumed with futility, your walk and your life will be futile. You will be doing things again and again that you know you shouldn't do, but you will do them anyway because it's what you always do. That's futility. It's realizing repeatedly that when you do what you always do, you make bad friends, you do stupid stuff, and you feel miserable afterwards. If your thinking pattern is futile, don't be surprised when your very best thinking gets you to acting as if life is futile. Albert Einstein is credited with a definition of insanity that fits futility perfectly: "Futility is doing the same things over and over and expecting a different result."

If your thinking runs along the lines of, *I don't have a way around this.* Think again. You are falling into a pattern of futile thinking. Just because you and I are Gentiles doesn't mean we have to keep thinking that way.

Futile thinking is not acceptable thinking if you're following Christ. This is the point the apostle Paul made as he continued his letter to the Ephesians, "They are darkened in their understanding, alienated from the life of God because of the igno-rance that is in them, due to their hardness of heart. They have become callous and have given themselves up to sensuality, greedy to practice every kind of impurity. But that is not the way you learned Christ!—assuming that you have heard about him" (vv. 18-21).

Have you heard how awesome Jesus is? Have you heard that God loves us and sent His Son? Have you heard that He died as an atoning sacrifice for your sin so that you can be completely forgiven to receive the free gift of eternal life? You can. That's called the good news—the gospel. You don't have to live under the weight of the consequences of futile, darkened thinking; you can be set free from all of that and step into the glorious liberty of the sons and daughters of Jesus through faith in Him. If you have never made the decision to turn from your sinful, futile thinking and trust Christ, you can make it today.

Let's back up and pick up the Bible text at Ephesians 4:20. "But that is not the way you learned Christ!—assuming that you have heard about Him and were taught in Him, as the truth is in Jesus, to put off your old self, which belongs to your former manner of life and is corrupt through deceitful desires and to be renewed in the spirit of your minds" (Eph. 4:20-23).

When Paul mentions the necessity that we "put off the old self," he is helping us understand how to remove sins from our lives. The picture is a worn out, flawed, old garment that represents our way of thinking. That painful but healthy process involves the following steps:

- First, we must relent. We must stop doing that sin and fix our sights on someone who loves us as we are and say, "You're right God about my sin."

- Second, we must repent. We experience the grief our disobedience and behavior causes and then admit, "I'm wrong, God."

- Third, we must remove. We take the source of sin to the street. Romans 13:14 is one go to verse on the practical preparations for thinking differently: "Make no provision for the flesh." Get serious about victory instead of sourcing your sin. If the equipment for sin and the environment for sin are readily available, you will find it very hard not to sin. I've already admitted I have no unfettered or unmonitored access to the Internet. I do this, not to limit myself, but to give myself real freedom!

As we have repeatedly emphasized in this series, our awareness of steps to deal with a problem isn't the same as taking the steps. Actually moving through the sequence of relent, repent, and remove breaks the cycle of futile thinking and puts us in a place to think differently.

I want to show you one verse in Genesis that nails this issue of sin removal. Genesis 4 records the immediate generational disaster caused by the invasion of sin into God's creation. Adam and Eve's children, Cain and Abel, had reached the age where worshiping God on their own was encouraged. Each brought an offering from their pursuits. Cain was enraged when his offering was rejected but his brother's offering was accepted. In Genesis 4:6 :"The LORD said to Cain, 'Why are you angry, and why has your face fallen?'" What a great question. God asked that question several times in the Bible, by the way (Isa.41:21; Jonah 4:4). If we're angry, once in a while God asks, "Why are you angry? Have you even thought about why you're angry?"

In Cain's case, the anger was written all over his face. God turned this into a great teachable moment: "If you do well, will you not be accepted? And if you do not do well [you know the rules], sin is crouching at the door. Its desire is for you, but you must rule over it" (Gen. 4:7). Cain had the chance to let his anger take its destructive, murderous course. Or, he could have chosen to think differently and relent/repent/remove. Because he did not decide to rule over sin, sin ruled over him. Cain discovered the crushing truth that sin not removed will inevitably return with a vengeance and ruin you.

What Cain faced is true for all of us. Sin is crouching at your door. We have an enemy who wants those strongholds protected and who intends to take our lives down. This is as real as real gets. You and I have to take radical action to relent, repent, and remove.

How are you keeping track of these crucial actions so that your mind is continually ready for the renewal work God wants to do?

Thinking differently and renewing your mind are the same thing, which then brings the crucial question: How do I renew my mind?

The answer to that involves these three mind-oriented disciplines to practice. This is the process of thinking differently. When you fail in the process, return to the crisis. So, if you're in any way serious about anything other than just going through the motions of the spiritual life, you will want to massively tune into the actions we will describe in the final three days of the study. This is the how to of thinking differently.

You may be thinking, *Do you have any evidence for the claim that renewing your mind and thinking differently are the same thing?*

Commit Romans 12:1-2 to memory: "I appeal to you therefore, brothers, by the mercies of God, to present your bodies as a living sacrifice, holy and acceptable to God, which is your spiritual worship. Do not be conformed to this world, but be transformed by the renewal of your mind."

Don't think like your sister; you are following Jesus. You don't have to think like your dad anymore; you have a Heavenly Father. He wants to give you the mind of Christ.

When Romans 12:2 says, "Do not be conformed to this world," we wonder how that can be avoided. The pressure is on, subtly and bluntly from every side, to conform to the way the world thinks. We want to think differently, but how does it happen? Paul tells us, "Be transformed by the renewal of your mind."

This is it. We are in the center of the bullseye. If you threw a dart and hit the bullseye of "how to change," and then I threw a dart after you which split your dart down the middle and hit "renewing your mind," that is the bullseye of "how you think differently."

DAY 3
PROTECT YOUR MIND

So how do you renew your mind? If you've posted a huge sign over your life that says "Mind Under Renewal," what activities can we expect to see going on in the way you think? If strongholds are surrounded by protection, doesn't it make sense to realize a sound and godly mind would also have some protective fences installed and some early warning systems in place to let us know there's something bad invading God's renewal project?

The first principle of mind renewal can be found in a familiar encounter recorded in Matthew 4:1-11 which reveals the significance of protecting our minds. The means of protection is found in the Word of God. You and I can guard our minds with the Scriptures. If we don't take that precaution, we will be vulnerable and defeated.

I'll assume that you opened your Bible to Matthew 4 when you saw it would be the text for today. Take a moment to read those eleven verses.

Matthew 4:1-11 is the story of the temptation of Jesus. Jesus was forty days in the wilderness, fasting and praying before His ministry. Just when Jesus was on the way out (It's always when we're the weakest, right?), Satan confronted Him and laid it down. When Jesus was desperately hungry, Satan confronted Him and launched his temptation attack.

Maybe there was a little sympathetic volley, "You look hungry there, bro. Have you forgotten who You are?" Then came the twisted challenge, "If you are the Son of God, command these stones to become loaves of bread" (v. 3). Where's the temptation? "You don't have to put up with this discomfort! You're more important and have more significant work to do than hang out in the desert starving to death. Taking care of this problem should be a piece of cake for you!"

Now Jesus could have answered this attack a lot of different ways, but He answered from the Word of God. Let's not forget that Jesus is the Word of God. And Jesus wrote the Word of God. But amazingly, Jesus answers from the Word of God and said these words: "But He answered, 'It is written, "Man shall not live by bread alone but by every word that comes from the mouth of God""'" (v. 4).

He had it. Of course He had it. He authored it. And He used it to crush Satan's first attack at multiple levels: He put bread in its secondary place, highlighted the life-giving nature of God's Word, affirmed the written record for His choice, and rejected the premise of Satan's attack ("If" you're the Son of God).

When the New Testament says in James 4:7, "Resist the devil, and he will flee from you," that passage doesn't mean to spar with the devil or go out looking for a temptation fight. The power to resist the enemy, and the means to protect your thinking, is wrapped in the power of the Word of God. That's why the lines from 2 Corinthians 10:3-6 have been constantly on our minds during these weeks. But, if the phrases from those verses didn't begin to flash in your mind when you read the text address because you have not even committed it to memory, you have significantly disadvantaged yourself.

Until you have those verses memorized you will not believe how often you will find yourself in a place of temptation or struggle and the Spirit of God will bring His Word to your mind. Now He has something to work with. When God reminds you to "take every thought captive to obey Christ," you will be able to say, "That's right. I don't have to fight with the flesh. This temptation must submit to the Son of God through the Word of God." You will have a powerful weapon, the sword of the Spirit, to protect your mind.

At the beginning of His ministry, Jesus had that weapon, and He used it. He kept it handy because His enemy and ours wasn't done. Satan came to Him a second time. "Then the devil took him to the holy city and set him on the pinnacle of the temple and said to him, 'If you are the Son of God, throw yourself down, for it is written...' Jesus said to him, 'Again it is written, "You shall not put the Lord your God to the test."'" (Matt. 4:5-7).

Satan tried to use Jesus' sword against Him. He twisted Scripture by ripping self-serving phrases out of context from God's Word to urge Jesus to take matters into His own hands and go for the big and impressive display of divinity rather than remaining the servant and Savior He came to be. There was a lot riding for us in Jesus' answer. He rejected Satan again with the Word, "Don't use My Word against Me to get Me to question My identity or purpose here!"

In an impressive way that ought to be a serious warning to us, Satan took a third run at Jesus: "Again, the devil took him to a very high mountain and showed him all the kingdoms of the world and their glory. And he said to him, 'All these I will give you, if you will fall down and worship me'" (Matt. 4:8-9). Satan was getting pretty desperate at this point because I can almost hear Jesus thinking, *So let Me just track with you here. You are going to give Me everything I created which is already Mine—if I bow down and worship you who I demoted from your job?*

But instead of direct engagement, Jesus dismissed Satan and said—and this is my point: "For it is written, 'You shall worship the Lord your God and him only shall you serve'" (Matt. 4:10).

Jesus could have spoken some new Scripture if He wanted to. So why didn't Jesus just make this another moment of revelation? I mean, when everything that Jesus says is the Word of God, why didn't He just author an answer in the moment? Why did Jesus quote the Bible? Because He was also showing us how to follow in His steps. While He is the Author of Scripture, and you and I are not, He is teaching us how to protect our minds.

How do you renew your mind? You begin by protecting it with the Word of God.

Take a few minutes to memorize and meditate on a powerful description of the protecting nature of God's Word. This is how David stated his case for the importance of uploading Scripture in his mind so that he would be able to think differently: "I have stored up your word in my heart, that I might not sin against you" (Ps. 119:11).

As you end, complete this prayer sentence: Lord, here are at least 10 reasons I love and am thankful for Your Word.

DAY 4
WASH YOUR MIND

Once you are making a regular practice of protecting your mind, it's time to continually cleanse the current bad stuff you discover in your thoughts by a process described as washing your mind in Ephesians 5:26.

You have to wash your mind with the cleaning agent of God's Word. In an extended passage on the larger picture God has created by the relationship between husbands and wives, Paul wrote the directive, "Husbands, love your wives, as Christ loved the church and gave himself up for her, that he might sanctify her, having cleansed her by the washing of water with the word" (Eph. 5:25-26).

The primary action in these verses is not what husbands are supposed to do; it's what Christ did. Because of what Christ did for His bride the church, husbands are commanded to do the same for their brides, not only because it's the right thing to do but also because it will serve to point others to what Christ has done on the cross to love, save, and sanctify His church. Sanctify means to make holy. In salvation, Jesus declares us to be holy; in sanctification, He is trying to make it so.

> **How's that going in your life? What evidences could you point to as examples of Christ's sanctifying and cleansing work in you right now?**

Ephesians 5:25-26 again says, "And gave himself up for her, that he might sanctify her, having cleansed her by the washing of water with the word." When you looked at the application question above you may have thought, *Sanctified? Me? I just don't feel all that sanctified. I have so many issues that leave me feeling mostly unclean.* But look at what Christ has done in making His Word available to us. In it we have the means for cleansing as we wash "with the word."

The Word is what washes our hearts and our thoughts. You may have heard some things, looked at some things, and done some shameful things. Like our hero,

Jacob, you may have some crippling regrets. But look at the advantage you have. Jacob didn't have a Bible. He didn't have what you have.

Luke 12:48 applies to our situation in powerful ways: "Everyone to whom much was given, of him much will be required." The washing capacity of God's Word is at our fingertips. But before we can saturate our minds with what He has written, we have to turn off the television, set aside our hobbies, and put everything on hold until we have made progress in immersing our thinking in God's Word. How will we know when we've washed enough? When we realize we are thinking differently!

Renew your mind by protecting it and washing it with the Word of God. By way of personal testimony, I would not be standing here if it were not for the sustaining power of the Word of God to right me, reconcile me with reality, and renew my thinking.

Washing your mind begins with continuous exposure. This is fairly elementary, so you can probably remember it after a single reading. This is the detailed washing with the Word procedure. Do these on a regular basis and you will be amazed at the way you find yourself thinking differently. Pick up your Bible and:

- **Read it.** Discover for yourself that different parts of God's Word will require different kinds of reading. The narratives will be easy to read like stories. Proverbs—you'll have to read and digest a verse at a time. Some sections will be slow going, but everything else God wants to do through His Word in you begins with the basic exposure of reading. You can add listening to it being read at this step also. Audio recordings of Scripture are a blessing.

- **Study it.** Get some tools like a study Bible, commentaries, a concordance that will help you track words used in various places in Scripture, and other aids. After you've read, observe what it says until you understand what it means. Then ask yourself what that passage requires of you.

- **Memorize it.** If you are doing the first two, you will probably find you're almost there. A verse or passage will become so familiar through repeated readings and study that you can visualize it without looking at the page. You want to upload as much Scripture to your mind as possible, so that you are able to transition to the next phase.

- **Meditate upon it.** Whatever else you're doing, and when you're stopped doing nothing, like being stuck in traffic, you can mentally scan through verses you've memorized, asking God's Spirit to illumine fresh understanding and bring new applications from Scripture to your life.

- **Share it with others.** This means telling others verbatim verses you are memorizing (helping them to do the same) and letting them know how your changed thinking and acting is flowing out of the impact of God's Word in your life.

  How many verses of the Bible could you quote right now from memory? Have you studied certain books in the Bible to the pont that you could reconstruct them from key verses? If you need a starting point, here are several powerful passages from God's Word about God's Word: Psalm 1:1-3; Psalm 19:7-11; Romans 11:33; 2 Timothy 3:16-17; Hebrews 4:12; 1 Peter 2:2.

Exposure to God's Word is always connected with benefits and rewards. God moves toward us when we wash our minds with what He has put into writing. Psalm 84:11 says, "For the LORD God is a sun and shield; the LORD bestows favor and honor. No good thing does he withhold from those who walk uprightly." You and I cannot walk increasingly uprightly without the Word of God renewing our minds.

The persistent practice of washing our minds with God's Word will have an impact on the relationships in our lives. Joshua 1:8 promises this centrifugal effect when Scripture is saturating the center of our lives: "This Book of the Law shall not depart from your mouth, but you shall meditate on it day and night, so that you may be careful to do according to all that is written in it. For then you will make your way prosperous, and then you will have good success." That first phrase "shall not depart from your mouth" is an interesting one to meditate on. It doesn't mean to not talk about it. It means, don't stop talking about it, ever.

When our lives are consumed with questions like, "Why can't I get any traction in my family?" or "Why can't I seem to get ahead in my career?" and "Why can't I get these temptations in the rear view mirror once and for all?" this verse in Joshua supplies an answer. You're not having good success because the great sin of your life is not that temptation as you see it. The great sin of your life is your neglect of the Word of God—and do all of the things you do while that Bible sits on the shelf. Remember, the Bible is life to you.

You may not be able to remember the last time you were directly challenged to make total exposure to God's Word the primary discipline of your life. This is it. Apart from an increasing dosage of God's Word, you will never think differently.

How many people have run a marathon and yet have never memorized a chapter in God's Word? How many people have built a successful business and yet have never memorized a psalm?

How many things (not necessarily bad things) have been higher priorities in your life than your intake of significant amounts of Scripture?

Between you and the Lord, you need to make some decisions about this today. What are some specific ways and times you are going to step up your interactions with God's Word?

Make this a matter of prayer today, not only for yourself but also for those in your study group pondering this same issue today.

DAY 5
SET YOUR MIND

The third aspect of the life-long process of renewing your mind with God's Word has to do with what Colossians 3:1-2 describes as setting your mind: "If then you have been raised with Christ, seek the things that are above, where Christ is, seated at the right hand of God. Set your minds on things that are above, not on things that are on earth."

Setting your mind is a point of saturation where your thinking is different because it is increasingly shaped by what God has said. Not in a wooden way, but in a way that demonstrates that Scripture does apply to living today, even with all the modern complexities that want us to think that no one has ever had to face such things before. The deeper we immerse ourselves in God's Word, the more we realize He had prepared for us a way of thinking that anticipates everything that we might encounter.

If you want to deepen your commitment to God's Word and set your mind on things above, there are three further actions you can make part of your spiritual training regimen:

- **Discipline.** Psalm 119:32 speaks to the increased capacity we have for God's Word if we will give ourselves to exposure consistently: "I will run in the way of your commandments when you enlarge my heart!" The habit of running increases all your functions, making your heart stronger and your lungs more efficient in handling air. The same principle follows ways we learn and obey all that we read in God's Word.

It's a conscious, deliberate practice. You have to do it like work, like getting on the treadmill. You understand discipline. You understand making yourself do something. I can tell you that (if you haven't done this) any day when you wake up and first think, *I know what I want to help me begin this day; I want God's Word* will be a good day. We may be used to wanting many other things in the morning, so wanting God's Word will have to move up in priority over time, but discipline will make it happen.

- **Desire.** Psalm 119:97 tells us that eventually the deliberate decisions and repetition of discipline will give way to desire: "Oh how I love your law! It is my meditation all the day." Somewhere in that window of time, I can just tell you (and this is a long time ago for me) that somewhere it moves from discipline to desire. What may seem like a willful choice to set your mind on things above will eventually be as natural as breathing and as necessary as feeding yourself good food. Any interruption will be noticed and even painful. It will feel like spiritual starving. But fortunately, if you are memorizing God's Word, there's always food in the pantry to feast on as you meditate. But there's more.

- **Delight.** Eventually, as Psalm 119:24 tells us, we can move beyond discipline and desire to genuine delight in God's Word: "Your testimonies are my delight; they are my counselors." Most of us find that the journey from desire to delight will be shorter than the journey from discipline to desire, but the whole trip will be worth it. When you begin to experience a range of emotional pleasures: relief, joy, satisfaction, contentment, wholeness, and many others in the simple act of opening God's Word, or turning from some distraction to meditating on Scripture, you will know you are in the territory of delighting in all that God has said.

My life verse is Jeremiah 15:16. When I was an eighteen-year-old kid trying to figure out what to do with my life, the Word of God came alive to me. "Your words were found, and I ate them, and Your words became to me a joy and the delight of my heart." At that age, I was all about appetites, but it took God's Word to get me under control and fill me with a continual appetite for Scripture. At my current age I see absolutely no reason to ever moderate my hunger for God's Word.

There is no thinking differently without the continual decision and practice of making God's Word central in our lives. Again, Colossians 3:2 tells us, "Set your minds on things that are above."

I like that picture of setting something. You know that if you're building something, the key is to finishing it is to set the nails that are holding everything together. At the close of his perceptive overview of life, Solomon said, "The words of the wise are like goads, and like nails firmly fixed are the collected sayings; they are given by one Shepherd" (Eccl. 12:11). He was talking about setting nails and setting our minds on God's Word.

"Set your minds on things that are above." That's what you do in the morning. When you get up and you have a day in front of you with a thousand decisions to make, feeling a ton of pressure, set your mind. Get up. Get into God's Word. Set your mind.

Now all that we've studied will flow into awesome life transformation with your commitment to renew your mind. And like something very small thrown into a racing rapid, this will all fade extremely quickly if you don't renew your commitment to be in God's Word by renewing your mind every day. The choice is before you, every day.

With everything we have studied together over these weeks in mind, allow me to conclude with a prayer over you as you cross the finish line of your assignments. May God richly bless your efforts to trust Him to help you think differently.

Pray with me:

Father, thank You, thank You, thank You for Your Word. It is such a generous gift. It is so perfect in all that it asserts. It is so healthy, and helpful, and feeding.

When I need comfort, You give it in Your Word.

When I need hope, You give it in Your Word.

When I need strength, You give it in Your Word.

When I need wisdom, You give it in Your Word.

Thank You, God, for Your Word. Please forgive our neglect of Your Word. Forgive my neglect of Your Word. Bring me, bring us, into a deeper season of digging into Your Word than we have ever known before, and I'm asking Lord, with deep gratitude, that we're not running across some vast chasm. No one in this study is shocked to hear me state that we need to give greater attention to Your Word so that our minds can be renewed—so that we can think differently.

Thank You, God, that this has been a healthy and holy priority in this group over these weeks. But make it only more so for our sanctification and for Your glory. In Jesus' name I pray, amen.

What's keeping you from your promised land?

In the newly updated study *Lord, Change My Attitude Before It's Too Late*, James MacDonald uses examples from the Israelites' journey out of Egypt to show that attitudes can affect whether someone stays in the wilderness or enjoys the blessings of the promised land. Learn how you can put off attitudes God hates and put on those He honors: from complaining to thankfulness, coveting to contentment, doubting to faith, and more.

Also from
JAMES MACDONALD

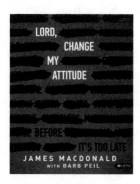

LORD, CHANGE MY ATTITUDE BEFORE IT'S TOO LATE
10 sessions

Learn how you can put off attitudes God hates and put on those He honors: from complaining to thankfulness, coveting to contentment, doubting to faith, and more.

Bible Study Book   005790073 $14.99
Leader Kit   005790074 $149.99

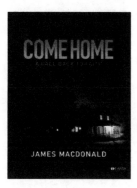

COME HOME
A Call Back to Faith
5 sessions

Develop a greater awareness of the disconnected and hurting, and equip believers to bring wanderers back to Jesus and the church.

Bible Study Book   005682240 $10.99
Leader Kit   005399890 $69.99

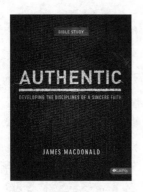

AUTHENTIC
Developing the Disciplines of a Sincere Faith
7 sessions

Learn to follow the example of Jesus by practicing the spiritual disciplines He used to maintain a close relationship with His Father.

Bible Study Book 005470535 $11.99
Leader Kit 005399891 $99.99

VERTICAL CHURCH
What Every Heart Longs For. What Every Church Can Be.
8 sessions

Get beyond a human-centered horizontal church to focus on seeking God's glory through worship, preaching, evangelism, and prayer.

Bible Study Book 005522647 $11.99
Leader Kit 005522646 $99.99

DOWNPOUR
He Will Come to Us Like the Rain
12 sessions

Take the personal steps you need to return to the Lord and experience spiritual renewal and victory.

Bible Study Book 001303830 $16.99
Leader Kit 001303831 $149.99

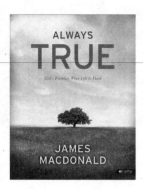

ALWAYS TRUE
God's Promises When Life Is Hard
6 sessions

Review universal promises based on biblical truths and principles, and learn that you can trust God to be faithful to His word no matter what you face.

Bible Study Book   005371573 $11.99
Leader Kit   005274675 $99.99

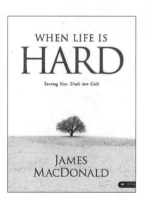

WHEN LIFE IS HARD
Turning Your Trials into Gold
6 sessions

Get very real, very practical answers straight from God's Word for encouragement and hope when enduring difficult times.

Bible Study Book   005293072 $11.99
Leader Kit   005271225 $99.99

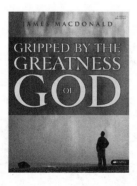

GRIPPED BY THE GREATNESS OF GOD
8 sessions

Discover the matchless attributes that characterize God—His sovereignty, holiness, grace, and glory—which naturally lead to a renewed heart of worship.

Bible Study Book   001288990 $12.99
Leader Kit   001288992 $149.99

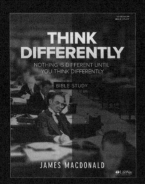

WHERE TO GO FROM HERE

We hope you enjoyed *Think Differently*. If so, please share it on social media with *#ThinkDifferently*. And now that you've completed this study, here are a few possible directions you can go for your next one.

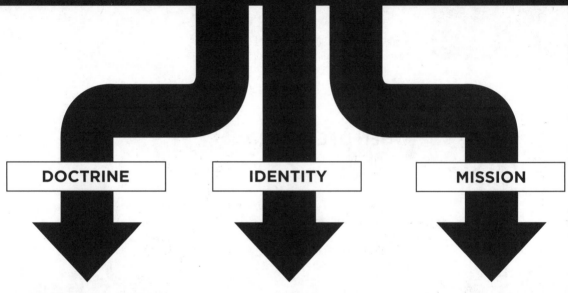

DOCTRINE

IDENTITY

MISSION

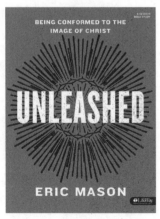

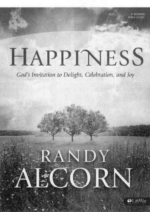

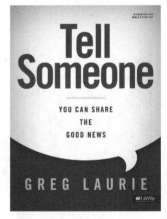

Get a better understanding of spiritual growth, and learn to maximize God's work to conform you to the image of Christ. (6 sessions)

Discover the indisputable proof that God not only wants us to be happy but also commands it. (6 sessions)

Realize the simple joy of evangelism as the good news of Jesus naturally overflows into your daily life. (6 sessions)

THINK DIFFERENTLY

NOTHING IS DIFFERENT UNTIL YOU THINK DIFFERENTLY

BIBLE STUDY

JAMES MACDONALD

Viewer Guides with Answers

Think Differently. Published by LifeWay Press®.
© 2016 James MacDonald. Item 005644087.
Made in the USA. Permission is granted to reproduce this item.

WATCH

Why is it so hard to change my thinking?

Because my battles are not primarily __physical__ (v. 3).

There are at least five major mental battles:

1. __Behavioral__
2. __Relational__
3. __Financial__
4. __Ideological__
5. __Moral__

Because my weapons are not readily __accessible__ (v. 4).

Our immediate tendency is to rely on __flesh__ weapons.

The weapons God provides for us have the following qualities:

They are __divine__.

They are __powerful__.

They __destroy__ strongholds.

Because my __strongholds__ are not easily __destroyable__ (v. 5).

My old __arguments__ made sense.

My old __opinions__ felt good.

My old __mind__ is opposed to __God__.

My old __pattern__ comes naturally.

Because my engagement must be __personal__ (v. 6).

WATCH

COMPLETE THE VIEWER GUIDE BELOW AS YOU WATCH DVD SESSION 2.

__Nothing__ is different until we think __differently__.

Strongholds are __fortified__ patterns of thinking that are stubbornly resistant to God's __Word__ and God's __will__ for us.

The three main sources of our strongholds are:

our __disposition__,

our __home__ __of__ __origin__,

and our __history__ and __habits__.

Everyone is born with a __disposition__ given to you by __God__.

__Disposition__ is the natural mental outlook, your predominant tendency or leaning, your prevailing point of view.

Disposition dictates my __thinking__ pattern.

Disposition affects:

my __pace__ -thinking,

my __people__ -thinking,

my __passion__ -thinking,

__all__ of my thinking.

4 DISPOSITIONS

DISPOSITION	MAIN FOCUS	NEEDS	DOWNSIDE
Choleric	Driver	Win	Aggressive
Sanguine	Expressive	Fun	Impulsive
Phlegmatic	Amiable	Safe	Passive
Melancholy	Analytic	Precision	Negative

4 DISPOSITIONS

DISPOSITION	TIME	AUTHORITY	PEOPLE PROBLEM
Choleric	Now	Rulers rule	Means to an end
Sanguine	Late	Majority rule	People pleaser
Phlegmatic	Tomorrow	Order rules	Not worth effort
Melancholy	Punctual	Rules rule	Beyond help

DISCUSS THE DVD SEGMENT WITH YOUR GROUP, USING THE QUESTIONS BELOW.

Which of the dispositions seems most like you? Since it's likely that you are primarily a combination of two of the classic dispositions, what's your runner-up disposition?

It's often easier to see the dispositions of others than to recognize our own. Discuss as a group who among you might fit each of the four categories: Choleric, Sanguine, Phlegmatic, and Melancholic.

How would you explain the difference between a personality strength and a stronghold?

In what ways do you think your disposition has shaped your faith and how you participate in your relationship with God?

Application: Seek to recognize at least one disposition stronghold you've developed. Take a few minutes with the group to pray with each other asking for God's help in learning to think differently during these weeks.

This week's Scripture memory.

> *We destroy arguments and every lofty opinion raised against the knowledge of God, and take every thought captive to obey Christ.* **2 CORINTHIANS 10:5**

Assignment: Complete the daily lessons for this week in preparation for the next group experience. Make a note of additional questions or thoughts related to this week's teaching that you can share with other group members. Pray for each member of your group by name, asking God to help them think differently.

WATCH

AS YOU WATCH DVD SESSION 3.

There are no __consequences__ for generational sins, but there are __inclinations__ .

Some of the most obvious generational strongholds:
1. __Substance__ __abuse__
2. __Materialism__
3. __Gluttony__
4. __Lust__
5. __Selfishness__

Exposing the bad decisions battles:
1. Where to __live__ —family vs. favorable?
2. Who to __marry__ —attraction vs. character?
3. __Peer__ group—easy vs. beneficial friendships?
4. __Leisure__ time—me vs. others?
5. Life __priorities__ —self vs. God?

WATCH

COMPLETE THE VIEWER GUIDE BELOW
AS YOU WATCH DVD SESSION 4.

Mind in Scripture can mean everything from __determination__ to __memory__.

The problem is that we can't change our __minds__ —can't __think__ differently— and can't destroy these strongholds until we know what they are.

Family of origin strongholds from last week:

1. __Generational__ __sin__ strongholds

2. __Conflict__ __resolution__ strongholds

3. Bad __decision__ - __making__ strongholds

Two more this week:

4. __Selfish__ __deceptive__ strongholds

5. __Money__ matters most strongholds

As James describes the strongholds, add notes in the margins about how what he says relates to your particular temperament and strongholds.

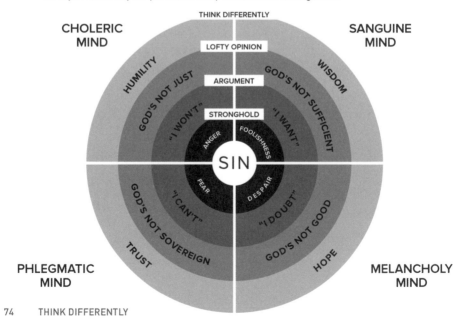

WATCH

Double-mindedness is wanting two things that can't __coexist__.

There are __double__-__minded__ people.

Double-mindedness creates __instability__.

Double-mindedness affects __everything__.

You have to __want__ to think differently.

Life is __10__ percent what happens to you and __90__ percent on how you choose to deal with/think about it.

Hope is the __confident__ expectation of something __better__ tomorrow.

Three reasons we stop hoping:

1. It's a __hassle__ to hope.
2. It's __hard__.
3. It __hurts__ to hope.

You have to take __action__ that __reinforces__ your desire.

WATCH

The most powerful driving force behind the strongholds that trip us up and take us down is our own __behavior__.

Strongholds show up when we __reap__ what we have __sown__.

One of the surest signs of a __stronghold__ is seeing __yourself__ in the sins of others.

The Stronghold Rule: Others will __do__ to you as you have __done__ to others.

Strongholds blow up through our own __decisions__.

Do any of the common 12 strongholds sound familiar? Check any that apply.

□ **Anger**	□ **False Guilt**	□ **Fear**
□ **Covetous**	□ **Rebellion**	□ **Unbelief**
□ **Control**	□ **Pride**	□ **Skepticism**
□ **Individualism**	□ **Idolatry**	□ **Escapism**

Jacob didn't have to keep __bargaining__ with God.

Jacob didn't have to keep __neglecting__ his family.

Jacob didn't have to keep __deceiving__.

Jacob didn't have to keep avoiding __conflict__.

Strongholds grow up in the __behavior__ of loved ones.

If nothing else scares us into __destroying__ the strongholds in our lives, seeing them in our __loved__ __ones__ should.

WATCH

Strongholds start to crumble when the consequences reach a __crisis__ point.

Eventually you get to the place in your life where God lets you feel the __full__ __weight__ of the choices that you have been making.

Five Strongest Strongholds:
1. Self-__righteousness__
2. Self-__deception__
3. Self-__loathing__
4. Self-__centeredness__
5. Self-__confidence__

Strongholds start to crumble when you finally get __time__ alone.

When we get alone:
1. __Demands__ cease.
2. __Distraction__ ends.
3. __Quiet__ invades.
4. __Reflection__ starts.
5. __God__ speaks.

Strongholds start to crumble when God __contends__ with you.

Strongholds start to crumble when God __prevails__ over you physically.

Strongholds start to crumble when God __marks__ you forever spiritually.

WATCH

COMPLETE THE VIEWER GUIDE BELOW
AS YOU WATCH DVD SESSION 8.

Some things we __cannot__ think differently about; some things we __must__ think differently about.

Strongholds: Those __fortified__ patterns of thinking that are stubbornly resistant to God's __Word__ and God's __will__ for us.

I'm not what I __could__ be; I'm not what I __should__ be, but I'm not what I __was__.

The most frequently used word in the Old and New Testament for this matter of changing your thinking and changing your mind is the Greek word *metanoia*, which means __repentance__.

Repentance is not a place we __visit__; repentance is where we __live__.

Repentance brings __cleansing__.

Repentance is a really __good__ thing.

Only __God__ can bring you to the place of genuine repentance.

Repentance: A __recognition__ of sin, followed by __heartfelt__ sorrow, culminating in a change of __behavior__.

Five Marks of Genuine Repentance:

1. __Grief__ over sin
2. __Repulsion__ toward sin
3. __Restitution__ toward others
4. __Revival__ toward God
5. A __future__ focus

WATCH

COMPLETE THE VIEWER GUIDE BELOW
AS YOU WATCH DVD SESSION 9.

Broken strongholds will battle to be __built__.

When you fail in the __process__ of thinking differently, you must return to the __crisis__ of stronghold repentance.

When you fall back, do these four things:

1. __Remove__ stronghold supports from your life.

Three Crucial Questions:
   a) Where did I go __wrong__?
   b) What __tripped__ me up?
   c) What needs to be __removed__?

2. __Reconcile__ your view of God with reality.

Six Faulty Views of God:
   a) God is a __killjoy__.
   b) God is a __prison__ __warden__.
   c) God is a __cranky__ boss.
   d) God is an __absent__ father.
   e) God is a __moody__ grandpa.
   f) God is a __scorekeeper__.

3. __Raise__ reminders to think differently.

4. __Review__ your identity and calling in God.

WATCH

Think differently or live to __regret__ it.

__Regret__ is when the verdict lands with finality: "I have no one to blame, but myself."

Real __relief__ is turning upward to __God__ , outward toward __others__ , and not inward to __self__ .

Express faith that confessed __weakness__ leads to __blessing__ .

Faith is __believing__ in the Word of God, __acting__ upon it, no matter how I feel, because God promises a good __result__ .

Jacob always bore the __scars__ of the strongholds he stubbornly maintained.

Thinking differently means __renewing__ your mind (Eph. 4:17-24; Rom. 12:1-2).

How to renew your mind:

1. __Protect__ your mind.

2. __Wash__ your mind.

Deepen your commitment to God's Word:

- __Discipline__
- __Desire__
- __Delight__

3. __Set__ your mind.